New Rig

Advancing Human Rights

Sumner B. Twiss, John Kelsay, Terry Coonan, Series Editors

New Rights Advocacy
Changing Strategies of Development and Human Rights NGOs

Paul J. Nelson

Ellen Dorsey

Georgetown University Press/Washington, D.C.

Library of Congress Cataloging-in-Publication Data

Nelson, Paul J., 1956-
    New rights advocacy : changing strategies of development and human rights ngos / Paul J. Nelson, Ellen Dorsey.
            p. cm.
    Includes bibliographical references and index.
    ISBN 978-1-58901-205-9 (cloth : alk. paper)—ISBN 978-1-58901-204-2 (pbk. : alk. paper)
    1. Non-governmental organizations. 2. Human rights. I. Dorsey, Ellen. II. Title.
    JZ4841.N33 2008
    323—c22   2007029598

15 14 13 12 11 10 09 08   9 8 7 6 5 4 3 2
First printing

Printed in the United States of America

Contents

Acknowledgments

This book has grown out of six years of discussion, research, conversations, consultancies, and classes, and it is not easy to assign credit (or blame) and acknowledge contributions adequately. Some of the present chapters were presented and discussed in earlier form, in panels at the 2004 and 2006 International Studies Association meetings in Montreal and San Diego, and at the 2004 meetings of the International Society for Third Sector Research in Toronto. Panelists and participants helped to shape our ideas, and we particularly thank Julie Mertus and Ken Conca.

We have had the benefit of discussion and comments on drafts of some of the book's chapters in seminars at the University of Pittsburgh's Graduate School of Public and International Affairs and at Carnegie Mellon University's Heinz School of Public Policy Management, and able research assistance from Srirak Plipat, Catherine Griebel, and Karolina Lyznik.

Colleagues in research and in the human rights and development fields have read and commented on portions of the manuscript and have been critical sounding boards, and we owe special thanks to Martin Staniland, Bret Thiele, Richard Claude, Curt Goering, Vienna Colucci, Jael Silliman, and Margaret Zeigler.

Parts of chapter 4 appeared as an article in the *European Journal of International Relations* in 2007, and the discussion of the Millennium Development Goals in chapter 3 draws on a 2007 article in *World Development*. We are grateful to the reviewers of those articles for critical comments that sharpened and challenged earlier versions. The authors, of course, are responsible for any errors of fact or judgment.

Finally, we would like to acknowledge our families, who showed tremendous patience and gave their support to this project. To Wallace and Demaris Nelson, Paola Scommegna, Renata and Ted Nelson; and to Martha and Joseph Dorsey and Anise Jordan-Dorsey, our thanks and love.

Abbreviations and Acronyms

AFL-CIO American Federation of Labor–Congress of Industrial Organizations

BIC Bank Information Center (Washington-based NGO)

CAFOD Roman Catholic relief and development agency, England and Wales

CARE CARE, formerly Cooperative Americans for Relief Everywhere

COHRE Centre on Housing Rights and Evictions

CRS Catholic Relief Services

EDF Environmental Defense Fund (now Environmental Defense)

ERI EarthRights International

ESC economic, social, and cultural (rights)

EURODAD European Network on Debt and Development

HRF Human Rights First (formerly Lawyers Committee for Human Rights)

HRW Human Rights Watch

ICCPR International Covenant on Civil and Political Rights

ICESCR International Covenant on Economic, Social and Cultural Rights

INGO international nongovernmental organization

IRN International Rivers Network

IRTK International Right to Know (campaign)

IWHC International Women's Health Coalition

LCHR Lawyers Committee for Human Rights

MOSOP Movement for the Survival of the Ogoni People (Nigeria)

MSF Médecins Sans Frontières (Doctors Without Borders)

MST Landless Rural Workers' Movement (Brazil)

NBA Narmada Bachao Andolan (Save the Narmada Movement)

NGO nongovernmental organization

RBA rights-based approach

SDI Slum Dwellers International

SPARC Society for the Promotion of Area Resource Centres

TAC Treatment Action Campaign, South Africa

UDHR Universal Declaration of Human Rights

Abbreviations and Acronyms

UNCED   UN Conference on Environment and Development
(Rio de Janeiro, 1992)
UNDP   United Nations Development Programme
UNICEF   United Nations Children's Fund
USAID   United States Agency for International Development
WEDO   Women's Environment and Development Organization
WSSD   World Summit on Social Development
(held in Copenhagen, 1995)

Introduction

L *ike slavery and apartheid, poverty is not natural.
It is man-made and it can be overcome and
eradicated by the actions of human beings. And
overcoming poverty is not a gesture of charity. It is an
act of justice. It is the protection of a fundamental
human right, the right to dignity and a decent life.*

—Nelson Mandela

Consider the following, seemingly disparate, activities of international nongovernmental organizations (NGOs):

- Oxfam International, known for its development, emergency, and global campaigning work, has adopted a rights-based approach as central to its organizational mission. Its "five aims" draw directly on internationally recognized human rights standards to advance the organization's development agenda.
- Save the Children has made the internationally recognized human rights of children the philosophical foundation for its work and the basis for operational decisions about programming and advocacy. Since its adoption in 1989 the Convention on the Rights of the Child has underpinned the work of the International Save the Children Alliance.
- Amnesty International voted in 2001 to transform the historic focus of the worldwide membership network's advocacy from largely a civil and political rights agenda to a new mission that encompasses economic, social, and cultural rights as well.
- In South Africa, Ghana, Bolivia, India, and dozens of other countries, human rights and constitutional guarantees are being invoked by opponents of privatization of drinking water systems, and international development and human rights

1

NGOs have joined in support of the human right to water movement.

- The Centre on Housing Rights and Evictions (COHRE) expanded its housing rights agenda to include training and education on all economic, social, and cultural (ESC) rights and active work on the human right to water.

- Human Rights Watch has begun to apply its investigative and reporting methods to documenting legal and institutional barriers to women's property rights in African countries along with a wider focus on discrimination in economic and social policies.

- The Brazil-based Movimento dos Trabalhadores Rurais Sem Terra (MST, Landless Rural Workers' Movement) has built an international network of peasant organizations, rural unions, development organizations, and international human rights NGOs, such as the Food Information and Action Network (FIAN), to advocate for agrarian reform as essential to the human right to adequate food.

- The Center for Economic and Social Rights, formed in New York in 1993, advocates for ESC rights in Ecuador, the United States, and the Middle East, and it helped launch a global network of NGOs on ESC rights. In 2003, NGOs from Africa, Latin America, and Asia met in Bangkok to form this new ESC rights network, uniting smaller organizations in the poor countries with a shared commitment to advancing ESC rights.

This book probes the extent, the significance, the limitations, and the interactions among initiatives such as these. These and the other organizations and movements profiled in this book share two central features: a concern for poverty and inequality and their worst symptoms; and a strategic interest in uniting human rights principles, standards, and methods with social and economic development. These examples embody three critical trends in NGO advocacy that are profoundly changing human rights advocacy and offering an alternative approach to economic and social development: (a) the embrace, sometimes tentative, of human rights–based approaches by influential development NGOs and donor agencies, (b) the adoption of active ESC rights agendas by major international human rights NGOs, and (c) the surge of work on economic and social policy through a human rights lens by specialized human rights NGOs and by NGO alliances and social movement campaigns. Taken together, these make up what we refer to as the "new rights advocacy." These new advocacy trends are also advancing "new rights"—new internationally recognized and increasingly codified human rights. This dual notion of new rights advocacy frames the following analysis.

Where did the human rights–development convergence come from, what drives it, and why did it emerge so rapidly in the late 1990s? What is the nature of change within and across the fields, and what are their implications for human rights and development theory and practice, for social movements, and for our understanding of NGOs and of the state?

To understand this convergence of activity in the development and human rights fields, we draw on perspectives from human rights, international relations, the sociology of social movements and of complex organizations, and development theory. We argue that changes in international systems have altered international NGOs' operating environment, forcing international NGOs to make strategic choices significant and widespread enough to change and reorient not only individual organizations but the fields themselves.

The systemic changes that drive the growing intersection of human rights and development are many and diverse, but at the core is poverty. Poverty and inequality are more acute and widespread in the mid-2000s than they were a generation ago, and they are more widely and prominently discussed. Reducing global poverty is the central goal of the Millennium Development Goals (MDG), endorsed at the turn of the millennium by 182 heads of state. Economist Jeffrey Sachs's (2005) bestselling book argues that the "end of poverty" is possible in our lifetimes, and even leaders of the global war on terror see extreme poverty and inequality as a key target in promoting security.

International agencies and scholars spin the numbers and debate methodologies (Wade 2004; Milanovic 2005; World Bank 2007), but there is general agreement that inequality among nations has grown over the past forty years, as has inequality within most countries, including fast-growing economies such as China and India. Inequality of income and wealth among individuals across the planet is enormous and growing; the incomes of the richest 5 percent of humanity equal those of the poorest 80 percent (Milanovic 2005). The number of people living on the equivalent of US$2 a day or less has stabilized and perhaps diminished in the first years of this century (World Bank 2007), but almost all the reduction is accounted for by employment and income gains in China's rapidly industrializing economy.

Women have fared disproportionately poorly under economic globalization's advance. Neoliberal development policies, advocated by many aid donors and often implemented by governments as a condition for assistance, have had a more severe impact on women and have undervalued women's work, disrupted their access to subsistence resources, privatized basic services, and reduced access to health and education essential for women's empowerment. These changes have decreased the number of women paid for work, increased inequalities in income and property ownership, decreased women's access to decision making, and increased the number of women living beneath poverty levels worldwide (AWID 2006).

For development agencies, the challenge and frustration are obvious: decades of concerted work have produced flashes of local success but a worsening global pattern of poverty, deepening inequalities, marginalization, and indignity. For many human rights activists, the failure to directly and meaningfully address the human rights dimensions of poverty became unjustifiable in the face of such suffering. Increasingly, the human rights field has challenged the human rights violations that fuel conditions of poverty: lack of access to adequate housing, water, and sanitation; poor health, discrimination, and marginalization in society; and patterns of labor, land ownership, and debt that trap individuals and societies alike in extreme inequality.

International NGOs and the national and local organizations and movements with which they work share a commitment to responding to deep and persistent poverty and inequality, to discrimination and marginalization of women and of disenfranchised populations, and to widespread disregard for existing legal protections in some societies. In the effort to become more effective and to assert greater power in national and international institutions, they are embracing human rights standards, methods, and rhetoric and expanding their human rights commitments to integrate economic and social with civil and political human rights.

Like many of the professionals in human rights and development whose work is the subject of this book, the authors have arrived at this perspective through their own work as scholars and practitioners. Approaching this subject from the perspectives of the two fields—steeped in the human rights movement and in development policy—we have ourselves experienced the movement in the two fields toward an approach to economic and social policy that draws on human rights standards and principles. We are also researchers trained in the social sciences and engaged in research on international development and international affairs, and contemporary theory on international relations, development, human rights, NGOs, and social movements appears unable to capture the changes we have participated in and studied.

Our research and teaching have also led us to explore how the two fields are challenging and changing each other. Over the years, our students in separate courses on human rights and on development and NGO management have pushed us up against the boundaries of the fields, asking why poverty is not a human rights issue or why the human rights to adequate food, to health, or to housing are not taken seriously in setting development priorities.

For the past five years, we have examined and documented changes in key organizations in the fields, scrutinized new programs and campaigns, and sought out the assessments of professionals in the fields. We have weighed the changes against models and theories in the research fields that try to capture and understand the significance of trends in development and human rights.

The changes we analyze here are occurring in diverse organizational settings and are typically studied separately by human rights scholars, organizational theorists, and international relations and development scholars. We draw on all these perspectives in an effort to account for the trends cutting across the fields. Why frame an inquiry into human rights in this way? We have become convinced that conventional approaches to human rights, NGOs, and development—their visions shaped by disciplinary and professional boundaries—are missing important changes that are most evident at the disciplinary boundaries and the organizational interstices, where human rights organizations, development funders, and social movements are increasingly in contact with each other. Among the significant theoretical and applied issues raised by this study, we highlight and introduce four here: the quest for power by NGOs reflected in their strategic choices, the origins and significance of new rights claims, the changing relationship between international NGOs and states, and the challenge to orthodox development theory and practice.

Power

How do we study power in the NGO sector? NGOs, we argue, rely on effective strategies, with clearly defined visions, to make maximum use of the sources of power they hold and to capture institutional power to advance their objectives. We want to understand more fully how NGOs respond to their environments by making strategic choices and how and where they mobilize sources of power in their efforts to influence larger, more powerful institutions. Scholarship on NGOs has tended to treat them either as principled, independent political agents advancing values-based agendas, or as organizations acting rationally to protect and perpetuate their own organizational lives. We start from the premise that international NGOs are, or can be, both political actors and rational organizations, and that to understand any NGO's behavior requires an integrated perspective that brings together complex efforts to exercise political power with equally complex organizational dynamics.

To understand these strategic choices and their collective effects requires understanding both the quest for power on the part of some international NGOs and the changes in their operating environments that necessitate new strategies. Especially in alliances and campaigns with social movements and activist NGOs from the poor countries, international NGOs' strategies are often designed to assert power in an effort to restrain corporate behavior or to support the demands of local or national movements in opposition to or support of state policy. At the same time, strategic choices have to be understood from the perspective of the organization and of its imperatives to survive, grow, and manage risk and uncertainty.

New Human Rights

Second, we know far too little about where new rights claims come from, how they arise and gain legitimacy and authority, and how the social and political dynamics of human rights claims really interact with the formal, legal life of human rights standards and principles. Our research focuses on the political and organizational life of international NGOs—major development and human rights actors based in the wealthy industrial countries—that influence the two fields at the global level. But we study international NGOs not only because of their own influence and significance, but because of what they can reveal about the exercise of power and the assertion of rights claims by social movements and by NGOs based in the poor countries. This idea that "new rights" are being created engages the second meaning of our title: fundamentally new rights are being advanced by human rights advocacy, arising out of struggles over social and economic conditions and policies.

Beyond the Violating State

Third, relationships between NGOs and the state in poor countries are changing in ways that scholarship on international relations and on NGOs has not yet captured. "Nongovernmental" has often been perceived as "antigovernmental," not only by suspicious government leaders and functionaries, but also by scholars and strategists who

observe the effectiveness of NGOs' invoking the authority of powerful states and international organizations to win compliance with
human rights standards. As international NGOs involved in policy
campaigns draw on economic and social human rights more systematically, they often find themselves in more complex and varied
relationships with governments, often supporting governments' pre-
rogatives in setting social policy while working to limit the authority
of international financial institutions and transnational corporations.
Yet they simultaneously maintain an oversight, monitoring, and dis-
senting role with governments.

These questions are of theoretical, conceptual, and applied significance. Theoretically, the complexity of these interactions presents a
challenge to existing models of NGO-state relations. For human
rights professionals, they raise challenges as well. Can an international standard of accountability for ESC rights be operationalized,
holding both rich countries and nonstate economic actors accountable for violations in specific third countries? Can NGOs simultaneously work in tandem with and in opposition to states without
undermining their own moral legitimacy? We argue that the ESC
rights experience compels us to create a more complex paradigm of
state-NGO relations that moves "beyond the violating state."

Challenging Neoliberal Development

Finally, the rise of human rights–based development approaches appears to challenge current and longstanding orthodoxy in development, and our study of development NGOs explores the nature and
significance of this challenge. Market forces' central role in development and the importance of limiting government interference with
the market have been features of development orthodoxy since the
early 1980s. Promoted by the World Bank, International Monetary
Fund, and some bilateral aid agencies, market-driven approaches
have been challenged by advocates of environmentally sustainable
development and human development, but these critics' concerns
have been integrated into a development orthodoxy that remains
market-driven.

A human rights–based approach to development, on the face of it, is more difficult to integrate with market-driven development. Unlike other countercurrents and slogans by development dissenters through the decades, rights-based development is grounded in a set of internationally accepted standards and principles that are in turn encoded in treaties, covenants, and international law. We want to understand how this countercurrent is being articulated among development professionals and how and whether it is shifting prevailing norms and practices to augment the influence of human rights. Conversely, we have investigated how the development industry is responding to rights-based initiatives and the risk that these initiatives could weaken the rigor and integrity with which human rights standards have been developed and promoted.

Adopting a broad, crosscutting, integrated perspective on human rights and development, the state, social movements, and international NGOs means embracing a subject that may seem hopelessly broad. Moreover, we are studying trends that are very much in process and the results of which are unpredictable and not yet determined. As a result, we cannot capture all the important evidence of trends among human rights and development NGOs and the social movements, international organizations, and government agencies with which they interact. We will instead highlight key developments that shed new light on the theory and practice of NGOs as political actors and as organizations, on the theory and practice of human rights, and on the theory and sometimes embattled practice of promoting economic and social development.

We have also narrowed the inquiry by focusing primarily on international NGOs, headquartered in the wealthy industrial countries and operating in three or more countries. (We refer to these as "international NGOs" and use other modifiers at times, including "southern NGOs" or "NGOs based in the poor countries," in an effort to be explicit about the kind of organization being discussed in a particular context.) Some scholars, particularly in development, have singled out international NGOs as innovators and have focused on them strategically because of their trend-setting roles (Lindenberg and Bryant 2001; Fowler 1997). We do find instances of such innovation, but in the movement toward an integrated approach to human rights and development, the lead has more often come from social movements and smaller NGOs based in the global South, where the promotion of human rights and social and economic development has for decades been more conceptually and organizationally integrated. International NGOs are important not as innovators but as globalizers, sources of support and legitimacy that adopt and convey new rights strategies among larger-scale transnational actors. Moreover, international NGOs have direct access to significant public constituencies in the wealthy industrial countries whose governments' activities in the global South are enormously influential.

The remainder of the book consists of four chapters and a conclusion. Chapter 1 lays out the theoretical significance of the new rights advocacy and traces its origins. Beginning with an analysis of organizational fields, which establishes the professional, social, and organizational dimensions of the historic separation of human rights practice and development practice, we trace some of the movements and interactions in the 1980s and 1990s that led human rights NGOs and development NGOs toward closer cooperation. With the prehistory of the new rights advocacy in place, the remainder of the chapters explain the theoretical and practical significance of the three trends that constitute the new rights advocacy and the four central questions these trends raise.

Chapters 2 and 3 trace the changes and trends of new rights advocacy through the human rights and development fields, respectively. Some of the most familiar names in development and human rights—CARE, Oxfam, Amnesty International, Human Rights Watch—are among the principals in the changes that are the focus of these chapters. There are important parallels between the trends analyzed in the two chapters, and each seeks to break down the elements of strategic and organizational change among international NGOs in the fields. But the differences between the patterns of change are equally important. NGOs in the two fields work in strikingly different organizational and professional cultures, display contrasting attitudes toward power, and build relationships with states that are based on sharply divergent working and political arrangements.

Chapter 4 turns to the political and organizational work occurring at the nexus of the human rights and development fields, where international NGOs interact with social movements and the state. It traces the interactions among international human rights, development, and environmental NGOs, community-based organizations, social movements, and grassroots campaigns on social and economic policy issues, beginning in the 1980s. We find that the number and intensity of exchanges and of changes in agenda and methodology grew as NGOs deepened their interaction across the human rights–development boundary. The implications of these changes are traced through the creation of new organizations, launching of new interorganizational initiatives across traditional divides, formation of alliances that involve leading NGOs in cooperation and dialogue, and the development of new rights campaigns in the late 1990s, in which human rights and development activists freely adopted and modified each other's methods and tactics.

We conclude in chapter 5 by revisiting the themes posed in this introduction: power and the strategies of NGOs, the rise of new rights claims, the changing relationship of international NGOs and the state, and the challenge to orthodox development theory and practice. To the longer-term questions of durability of the changes and their impact on the success of human rights and development strategies, we are able to provide partial answers. Durability is a subject we will return to in the conclusion.

The trends analyzed here are new, and they require rigorous conceptual treatments to categorize seemingly disparate activities in organizational fields with very different traditions. They also demand careful empirical research that creates baseline data to allow for tracking of impact over time. Our efforts here are first steps, characterizing the new trends themselves, identifying new theoretical frameworks for analyzing these trends, and analyzing their potential benefits and risks, while raising key questions for future research. But the fact that this early effort to clarify the human rights–development interaction is necessarily modest in scope does not diminish the profound significance of what has been happening in the two fields. The obvious significance lies in the changes adopted by the NGOs themselves, often requiring fundamentally new approaches and understanding for staff members, volunteers, and donors. But its greatest significance lies in the potential for success and risk of failure. The global challenge of meeting social and economic needs has grown in unprecedented ways. Changing strategies is risky business but perhaps essential.

1

NEW RIGHTS ADVOCACY

Despite our growing global base of financial and
human capital, increasingly sophisticated
technology, and the experience of decades in
international cooperation, poverty, inequality, and
repression continue to fuel security threats both within
societies and across borders. Globalization, although
making good on certain of its promises to generate
higher rates of economic growth, confers the vast
majority of its benefits on a chosen few.

—Louise Arbour, United Nations High Commissioner for
Human Rights

The curious separation of human rights and development began immediately after the drafting of the Universal Declaration of Human
Rights, when cold war politics thwarted efforts to forge one treaty
legally binding upon government signatories. Civil and political
rights and economic, social, and cultural rights were bifurcated along
the political fault lines of the period, and different treaties and mechanisms were created to promote them through the United Nations
system.

In the 1960s, with the founding of new international human rights
NGOs, advocacy on behalf of civil and political rights worldwide began in earnest. Development emerged as a field during the same period. The World Bank began lending in 1948, and the field grew
slowly in the 1950s but more rapidly in the 1960s, accelerating in the
1970s and 1980s until by 2000 development assistance was a $64 bil-
lion annual enterprise. Except in rarefied debates in the United Nations, official development was devoid of references to economic and

13

social human rights, and the two fields proceeded on separate conceptual tracks through parallel sets of intergovernmental institutions.

But by the 1990s development was in crisis and human rights NGOs were facing dramatically changed conditions. Trends and forces created powerful incentives for development and human rights, separated almost at birth, to begin to reunite. The dynamic interaction that ensued between human rights and development is the story of this book. Since the mid-1990s the human rights movement has begun to take seriously the economic and social rights guaranteed in the international human rights covenants; development and human rights NGOs have joined in human rights–driven social movements for food, health, education, water, and other rights, often challenging development orthodoxy; and development organizations have adopted "rights-based" approaches to their work. Collectively, these three trends signal a concerted effort to bring the norms of economic and social human rights into the mainstream of world politics, as human rights advocacy in the 1960s and 1970s legitimated political and civil human rights.

We begin our analysis of these trends by introducing the idea of organizational fields and providing an account and analysis of the historically separate development and human rights sectors. Next we turn to the impact of international system change on strategies of international NGOs. We argue that these changes alter the operating environment for international NGOs and compel them to adopt new strategies and methods of operating. Our account of these changes in strategy is the basis of the rest of the book, in which we analyze the trends that are breaking down some of the sector divisions and demonstrate how sectors and prominent international NGOs are opting for new and broader mandates and agendas.

The remainder of this chapter introduces four key theoretical debates addressed in our analysis. First, we analyze the dual identity of international NGOs. It is essential to recognize that they are international political actors, but they are also organizations, driven by organizational imperatives to survive, protect themselves from uncertainty, and conform to social myths and expectations. Second, we offer an interpretation of the debate over the nature of human rights, on one side the legal positivist approaches that give priority to international treaties and the juridical mechanisms created to implement them, and on the other side approaches that see rights claims as arising out of social movements' efforts to assert power or limit the powers of states and other actors. We argue that while new human rights claims have arisen out of social movement mobilization, legal codification of the standards is critical to achieving sufficient power to influence national and international policy decisions.

Third, we argue that the relationship between NGOs, human rights, and states requires rethinking in light of the new rights advocacy. NGOs' frequent adoption of strategies that go beyond identifying the violating state alone, and that in some instances seek to shore up, rather than limit, states' policy options, leads us to offer a new model for international NGOs as political actors. Fourth, we consider the implications for development theory, which has historically been a theory of economics, markets, and institutions, but not one of economic or social rights and entitlements.

At the conclusion of the chapter we return to the diversity of the organizational fields to observe the divergent ways international development and human rights NGOs confront trends in the international political economy and embrace human rights themselves.

Organizational Fields and the Division of Human Rights and Development

The two new organizational fields grew along separate tracks, and the clear division of institutions, professional skills, and organizational cultures runs through the UN system, foreign affairs and international development agencies of most of the bilateral aid donors, and profoundly through the world of NGOs. From the end of World War II to the mid-1990s, "human rights," "development," and "environmental" operated in distinct organizational fields, distinguishable by their organizational missions and agendas, patterns of association, funding, disciplinary affiliation, and organizational cultures and myths. They share certain strategic priorities, but they have largely operated in parallel, strategizing around related but seldom overlapping agendas, drawing financial support from distinct sources, and maintaining primary relationships with distinct sets of government offices and grant makers.

To grasp the differences between their methods and cultures, one need only reflect on the two most visible and memorable symbols of major international NGOs during the period: Amnesty International's barbed wire and candle and the "CARE package." One logo symbolizes citizen action to light the flame of hope and redress human rights violations, and the other a humanitarian response to alleviate acute human misery. But the symbols are more than contrasting logos. They also imply different methods and objectives, with human rights groups building an international community of trained investigators and activists to pressure for change, and development organizations soliciting financial support for community development projects or emergency relief, and mobilizing advocacy campaigns targeting primarily aid donors.

These organizational fields are most clearly demarcated at the international level. Their influence makes international NGOs interesting, but it is important to note that the division between sectors is not universal. While international NGOs have historically operated in distinct sectors, human rights and development activists in the poor countries have worked together to develop strategies to respond to the changing world political economy. This is a theme we will return to in each chapter: as NGOs begin to grow rapidly in the countries of the global South in the late 1980s and early 1990s, they have an impact on the methods and outlooks of international NGOs in both development and human rights.

Organizational fields are recognized by their intensive interaction, shared recognition of a common identity and common purpose, and practice of cooperation as well as competition as evidence of their involvement in a "shared endeavor" (Dimaggio and Powell 1983). Consider three of the core characteristics for development and human rights NGOs summarized in table 1.1: their allegiances, professional ties, and core methodologies. Human rights NGOs articulate their agendas and missions in terms of strengthening international human rights norms and protecting and implementing recognized human rights. Most human rights NGOs have focused on civil and political rights, and largely on the conduct of governments. They associate with UN and governmental human rights agencies and offices and with other human rights NGOs, and they receive much of their funding from private donors and foundations. Although their methodologies vary, the core activities of human rights advocacy are promotion of standards, investigation and documentation of violations, advocacy, and litigation (Welch 2001). Taken together, these are the core of the "mobilization of shame" methodology (Drinan 2001).

Development NGOs have a different normative base and methodology. Their agendas seldom make reference to any fixed standards, but refer to meeting human needs and promoting self-sufficiency, community development, or justice. Their dominant activity has

Table 1.1 International NGO Fields and Their Core Characteristics

	HUMAN RIGHTS	DEVELOPMENT
Mission	Promote and protect internationally recognized human rights; document and encourage action to redress violations	Advance well-being and dignity of vulnerable groups; respond to emergency needs
Allegiances, standards	Internationally recognized standards: civil and political, economic, social and cultural human rights	Meeting basic human needs, promoting human development; cost-effectiveness; popular participation
Methods	"Mobilizing shame"; investigation and documentation; HR education; advocacy as core activity; litigation; partnerships as solidarity	Mobilizing compassion; programs and projects with time horizons; advocacy complements services; partnerships as capacity building; emergency relief
Resources	Foundations; individual memberships	Donor governments; individual members; foundations
Professions	Legal profession and social disciplines, especially political science, area studies	Economics, social disciplines, area studies, agronomy, public health, engineering

been the delivery of material goods or services (roads, immunizations, organizational capacity building) in poor societies, although
policy advocacy is now increasingly important to their agendas. They
interact with development aid donors and organizations involved in
community development and are funded largely by private donors
and governmental aid agencies (Lindenberg and Bryant 2001).

International NGOs in the two fields rely on different means of
social legitimation. Development organizations' legitimacy is derived either from (a) a methodology that assures agencies and their
publics of "impact," cost-benefit analysis, or another measure of economic impact, or (b) from relationships, as in the case of NGOs that
support cooperatives, trade unions, chambers of commerce, or indigenous peoples' organizations. Human rights NGOs' legitimacy,
however, rests on internationally recognized standards and principles, anchored in respect for human dignity and codified in international law, that they promote and defend. Technical expertise,
rigorous impartiality, and other attributes are important but secondary sources of legitimacy.

The two fields have remained largely separate and parallel throughout their history. The International Covenant on Economic, Social
and Cultural Rights (ICESCR), along with declarations of the Right
to Food and Right to Development, have been debated in international conferences and UN committees, but aid agencies have rarely
seen rights as a source of guidance when allocating funds or designing projects and programs (Gauri 2004). Civil and political human
rights sometimes influence governments' aid allocation (Forsythe
2000), but broadly speaking, across the decades in which "development" and "human rights" have come of age, they have been separate and largely uncoordinated.

But development and human rights international NGOs are changing their methods and approaches to respond to the effects of economic globalization. They are collaborating in advocacy campaigns,
adopting and adapting each others' strategies, and adopting new
methods that cross historic dividing lines: human rights advocacy for
development and environmental NGOs and an expanded spectrum

of human rights advocacy for traditional human rights groups. Collectively, we refer to these changes as the new rights advocacy.

The New Rights Advocacy

We define the new rights advocacy as advocacy on social, economic, or development policy, at local, national, or international levels, which makes explicit reference to internationally recognized human rights standards. It features explicit appeals to these standards, it promotes both civil and political human rights and economic and social human rights, and it targets a broad range of actors.

We use the term "rights" advisedly. Human rights scholars and activists traditionally insist that the full term, "human rights," be used, and have sometimes been disturbed by development practitioners' reference to "rights-based" approaches, implying or asserting that they select from among the recognized human rights as fits their programmatic needs. Oxfam International (2002a), for example, has distilled five "aims," expressed in terms of rights, which govern its agenda setting and define its rights-based mission. These adaptations of rights to fit organizational agendas are discussed in more detail in chapter 3. We adopt the term "new rights advocacy" not to take sides in this discussion—indeed, we would side with the protectors of the "human rights" usage—but because it best captures the breadth of new, politically significant activity that is tied to the power of these human rights.

New rights advocacy is a dual concept, and both of its levels of meaning are important to our argument. New rights advocacy refers first to concrete activity among actors in the two fields: the embrace of ESC rights among human rights activists; the adoption of human rights–based approaches in the development field; and the formation of new advocacy campaigns, networks, and movements that involve organizations from both fields as well as social movements. These three trends are the focus of chapters 2, 3, and 4. But a second level of meaning is intended as well, one that is more literally about "new rights" and new claims of human rights. In the late 1990s and the first years of the new millennium, new substantive rights (e.g., to water) have been claimed and recognized, and advocates have asserted new, specific implications of broader human rights in ways that strengthen advocacy claims (e.g., right to agrarian reform, right to access to essential medicines), claims that have arisen in the context of the changing patterns of human rights advocacy.

In its first sense, new rights advocacy refers to three interrelated trends. The first trend is the move by traditional civil and political rights NGOs to cover ESC rights, exemplified by Amnesty International's adoption of a new mission that goes beyond its historic civil and political mandate, Human Rights Watch's work on discrimination patterns in economic and social policy, and Human Rights First's efforts to integrate ESC work in its cooperation with southern counterpart NGOs.

The second trend is the adoption of rights-based approaches to development by existing development, environment, and labor groups. International development NGOs such as CARE, Oxfam, ActionAid, and *Rädda Barnen* (Save the Children Sweden) are implementing "rights-based" approaches that parallel the move by official development agencies, from UNDP and the UN Food and Agriculture Organization (FAO) to the Swedish and British bilateral aid agencies, to implement rights-based methods in their own programming.

The growth of new movements and organizations that explicitly link human needs issues to social and economic rights standards—as in campaigns for essential medicines, right to water, and women's reproductive health rights—is the third component of the new rights advocacy. Among the leading international NGOs advancing economic and social rights as their core mission are the Center for Economic and Social Rights, Centre on Housing Rights and Evictions, Food Information and Action Center, and the International Women's Health Coalition.

As such organizations have proliferated at the global, regional, and national levels, they have often been led and even challenged by national NGOs in the poor countries, with agendas already dedicated to ESC rights. The Nigerian Social and Economic Rights Action Centre (SERAC), the Indian Tamil Nadu Network for Economic,

Social, and Cultural Rights, and the Brazilian Institute of Social and Economic Analysis (IBASE) are prominent examples of this movement among NGOs in the poor countries. Many such NGOs are now linked in an International Network for ESC rights, founded in Bangkok in 2003 (see www.escr-net.org).

Aspects of these three trends have appeared earlier within individual NGOs, sometimes for decades. Save the Children, for example, was founded in England in 1919 with an explicit commitment to the rights of the child, and it has worked throughout its history to secure international agreements on these rights, even as it delivered services directly to children and their families. The Food Information and Action Network (FIAN), the Hamburg-based NGO for the right to adequate food, has existed since 1984, the IWHC since 1983. What is new is the scope of the embrace and the scale of change occurring in each sector, the adoption or serious discussion in the UN system and in many important international NGOs in the late 1990s, and the effect their simultaneous adoption is having on interactions between the sectors. This new surge of interest has been triggered, we argue below, by four major changes in NGOs' external operating environment that force NGOs to reconsider how they carry out their stated principled mission and how they survive and flourish in an increasingly competitive sector.

For individual international NGOs, the experience is often new in other ways, bringing new policy issues, new advocacy strategies and tactics, new alliances, and often new organizational methodologies, which compel fundamental changes in how work is accomplished. Although the changes in method and networking are new for international NGO participants, it is important to note that some southern NGOs have quietly practiced these integrated strategies for more than a decade.

But new rights advocacy also refers to the fact that new claims to human rights are being made, and new forms of advocacy are being used to advance them. New claims include claims to specific economic and social goods, such as the human right to water, the right of access to essential medicines, the right to agrarian reform as a prerequisite to achieving the right to adequate food. The emergence of these claims from the demands of social movements is documented in subsequent chapters. For the present, we turn next to the systemic changes that are driving this reorientation of human rights and development.

International System Change and the NGO Sectors

In the past twenty years, there has been an explosion of research and analysis of NGOs and transnational social movements. The surge of organizing and activity has been attributed to failures of traditional channels of political participation, to discredited ideologies of liberalism and Marxism, to new technologies, and to the logic of global governance, by which transnational networking is required to put in place solutions to inherently global problems.

Much of the NGO literature examines the functions and methods of NGO activity and (less thoroughly) their impact on policy outcomes, and a rich body of literature on NGO influence with international organizations, national and local governments, and global economic actors has been accumulated (Florini 2000; Edwards and Gaventa 2001; Fox and Brown 1998; Wapner 1996). Scholars and practitioners increasingly probe NGOs' limitations, raising questions of duplication of resources and mandates, competitive agendas, resource dependence, cooptation to government and corporate agendas, and issues of legitimacy and accountability to their constituent bases (Weiss and Gordenker 1996; Rieff 1999; Slim 1997; Ebrahim 2005).

Several recent studies have focused on North-South relationships among NGOs involved in advocacy campaigns. Weaknesses in the accountability of international NGOs to the national and community organizations in the poor countries have been the subject of studies of advocacy of the World Bank (Nelson 1996; Fox and Brown 1998), the environmental movement (Roe 1995), in human rights (Guilhot 2005), in movements such as the debt relief/debt cancellation movement (Keet 1999), and in decision making about development assistance (Fowler 2000a) and advocacy (Jordan and van Tuijl 2000, 2006; Bob 2005).

Development theorists monitor the interactions of NGOs with multilateral and bilateral aid programs and policies, and the human rights field has produced a wealth of studies of NGOs and their role in norm setting at the United Nations (Gordenker and Weiss 1996) and other intergovernmental organizations, and in shaping corporate conduct and governments' human rights practices (Newell 2000; Wapner 1996; Risse-Kappen 1995; Risse, Ropp, and Sikkink 1999; Clark 2001; Welch 2001).

Analysis of transnational social movement campaigns has also proliferated, focusing on the anti-apartheid movement, the nonproliferation treaty campaign, the global women's movement, and the international campaign to ban land mines, to name a few (Dorsey 1992, 2002; Edwards and Gaventa 2001; Mekata 2000; Tarrow 2005; Della Porta and Tarrow 2005). These studies document the role of specific NGOs operating in a web of coordinated action to achieve predetermined and specific goals.

International relations theory has taken an interest in NGOs as political actors and independent variables in accounting for policy change. Keck and Sikkink's (1998) widely discussed account of transnational advocacy networks, and numerous variants on that model, all focus on the roles that NGOs and other principled, values-driven actors can play, often organized in networks, to induce changes in state policy or in influential international rules and norms. Our argument in this book does engage these ongoing debates from the NGO and social movement literature. But first and more fundamentally, we are posing a new question: Have changes in the international systems—the rules, institutions, and relationships that order power relations among states and other actors—produced recognizable changes in NGO sectors' methods, missions, and strategies?

Research in development, human rights, and international relations has examined NGOs' efforts to change state policy, and although the findings have not produced a consensus about the importance and independence of NGOs' impact, the evidence is mounting for some influence, at least under certain conditions (Price 2003). It is also nearly axiomatic in international relations that change in international systems—physical, financial, economic, geopolitical—in turn changes state policy (Buzan and Little 1994). Whether this causal link is mediated by states' calculation of their own interests alone, by the need to alter the institutions of interstate cooperation, or by a challenge to states' construction of their interests, opportunities, and threats, international system change is a fundamental force driving changes in state policy.

The 1990s brought significant shifts in power from the classic state-centric model of an international system toward one with multiple economic and social movement actors interacting with states and influencing international system dynamics (Held 2004). What remains to be systematically explored is how international systems change affects NGO sectors' strategies. The strategy of NGOs acting in a field such as human rights or development is, in a loose sense, analogous to state policy in that it involves calculated responses to systems changes that can pose threats and opportunities. We hypothesize that international systems change is causing fundamental changes in the development and human rights international NGO sectors. Note that we refer to entire fields of NGO action. What is at issue is not the easy question of whether individual NGOs make new strategic choices in the face of systems change; they surely do. The question is whether there is evidence that the entire field is being reoriented, undergoing what could be called a paradigmatic change.

The question requires us to think systemically about the NGO organizational fields—human rights, environment, development—their policy objectives and methods, and the international conditions that affect them. Few will dispute that international systems have changed dramatically over the past twenty years. The end of the cold war, creation of new international trade and finance regimes and rules, increased capital mobility and influence for international corporations, growth of new and diffuse threats to human security, and the growing transnational organization of social movements and NGO campaigns are among the most significant changes and trends. We anticipate that these changes will produce not merely adjustments in tactics, programs, and priorities for individual NGOs, but a broader reorientation of NGO fields.

International NGOs struggle to maintain the independence, credibility, and stability that are essential preconditions to the exercise of power and influence, and NGOs in both fields also search for ways to gain greater leverage in their relations with states and international organizations. Changes in international systems with corresponding changes in power relations, we hypothesize, affect NGOs' operating environment decisively enough to shake up these strategies and force NGOs to consider new strategies. The influence on international NGO strategies is felt in two ways: through changes that affect the success or failure of NGO programs, and through changes that create changed expectations or new pressures on NGOs' surviving and flourishing as organizations. The relationship is represented graphically in figure 1.1.

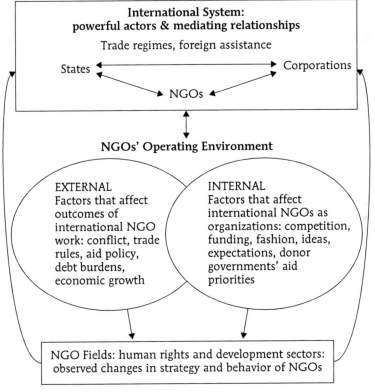

Figure 1.1 *International Systems, Operating Environments, and International NGOs*

Organizations, Their Environments, and Power

What changes in the global environment are driving the convergence of human rights and development organizations? Although the factors vary somewhat for the two sectors, as we will see below, the move is motivated by changes at both the global and local levels that create incentives for development NGOs to move toward human rights–based strategies and methods, and incentives for human rights organizations to embrace ESC rights advocacy.

We will first briefly outline the major changes in the international system, in the 1990s and continuing to today, that have made human rights and cross-sector cooperation more attractive to both human rights and development NGOs. These include the four outlined here: trends in trade and globalization, social movement organizing, official aid policy, and conflict and humanitarian crises. With this framework established, we will then turn to the global and local events through which international NGOs experience these systemic changes. These events are many and varied, but here we introduce the two sets of events that are analyzed in chapter 4: controversial large-scale development projects and the UN-sponsored global conferences of the 1990s.

Four changes in the global environment have challenged development and human rights NGOs in every major dimension of their work. Two of these, globalization and the growth of new social movement solidarity, are among the most fundamental changes facing NGOs. The rapid globalization of trade and finance and the expanding powers of transnational corporations now raise the possibility that corporations may be as likely to be the direct agents in violating human rights standards as governments and that decisions made in major corporate boardrooms are often more significant for the course of development than policy decisions made by national development planners.

Alongside the growing integration of global capital have come new forms of international mobilization among social movements and organizations of students, consumers, women, indigenous people, and others concerned with the growing power of corporations.

These movements sometimes directly challenge NGOs in both sectors, as in protests at the World Trade Organization (WTO) or G-8 meetings, or when movements for agrarian reform or for the right to water compel international NGOs to decide whether and how to follow the lead of more radical poor people's organizations. Pressure from NGOs operating in the poor countries or from radical social movements has also created conditions for new alliances or cooperative campaigns involving international NGOs. At other times social movement mobilization poses an indirect challenge by compelling international NGOs to consider shifting strategies to compete for the membership and loyalty of young activists and donors. The popularity of the antisweatshop movement on U.S. college and university campuses, for example, was an important environmental change for Amnesty International USA and Oxfam America, both of which emphasize campus organizing and recruitment as an important source of activist supporters and members.

The reductions in official development assistance and shifts in its allocation toward geopolitical hot spots have confronted international development NGOs with fundamental questions about their resources and their place in the global aid system, questions that are discussed in chapter 3. These pressures are compounded by the explosion of conflict and complex humanitarian situations worldwide since 1980. Despite donor commitments to expanded aid, the World Bank's *Global Development Finance* report acknowledges that net official flows from donor countries declined from 1990 to 2004 from just over $50 billion to just over $25 billion (World Bank 2005). For international development NGOs, aid allocations are both a critical part of their own organizational operating environment and an important subject of their advocacy agenda.

Conflict-related humanitarian crises have heightened the pressure on NGOs in both sectors. Since the early 1990s, human rights NGOs have raised questions and forced humanitarian practitioners to confront more directly the possibility that humanitarian assistance may prolong conflicts, fall into the hands of combatants and flagrant human rights abusers, and in some circumstances contribute more to human suffering than it relieves. These discussions, together with several insightful but sometimes unflattering portraits of humanitarian relief agencies during the period (Sogge 1996; Barrow and Jennings 2001; Middleton and O'Keefe 1998), have stimulated discussion about how humanitarian law and human rights standards may help guide the management of relief operations (Terry 2002). The experience of humanitarian assistance is discussed further in chapter 4; for the present, the important effects of conflict-related crises are to push humanitarian (and development) NGOs toward international human rights rules and international humanitarian law and to draw international human rights NGOs into closer contact with the messy business of humanitarian response and relief.

These shifts in global systems produce new trends within the NGO operating environment, yet they affect development and human rights NGOs differently as fields and provoke a variety of strategic responses from individual actors. Although there are common experiences and factors in the global political economy that affect organizations in the two sectors, the defining events for the sectors are to some extent different. In the development sector, the trend that shapes the current human rights challenge is the rise to dominance of neoliberal economic principles and policies in the 1980s. If structural adjustment, with its inconsistent and often painful impacts in the poor countries, was the turning point in the recent history of development, the end of the cold war played a similar role in the human rights sector. Cold war divisions were the political and historical origins of the split between the civil and political rights covenant and the ICESCR. Much of this book's three central chapters—on development, human rights, and the alliances and hybrid organizations that bridge the sectors—analyzes changes in the organizations in these sectors.

NGOs experience these changes in the operating environment through changing relations among actors and the surfacing of new constraints and opportunities, both political and organizational. But global systems are abstractions, and to observe the link between systems change and the strategic orientation of international NGO fields we must identify the observable events through which international NGOs encounter and respond to change.

The Emergence of NGO Cooperation in the 1980s and 1990s

Economic globalization, social movement pressure, changes in official aid, and conflict-related humanitarian crises provide the framework for understanding why the development–human rights convergence began to grow in the 1990s. The early stages of the contact, beginning in the 1980s and first half of the 1990s, form a prelude to the new rights advocacy and lay the foundation for the emergence of new strategies that are the story of chapters 2 through 4.

Locally based battles over large-scale development projects in the 1980s and 1990s, and the series of global conferences and negotiations of the 1990s, have been well documented. But they are significant for the human rights and development fields in a way that has not been much discussed: they brought together practitioners and activists in the local and international arenas, from the development, human rights, labor, and environment sectors, and from the global women's movement and indigenous peoples' movement, and they laid the foundations for the human rights and development convergence described in the remaining chapters.

Whether and how these movements, meetings, and protests affected policies and institutions is an important and separate question, but it is not our primary concern. What interests us is how individuals and organizations in human rights and development were repeatedly brought into contact with each other.

Contact between the fields deepened in a variety of ways. Individuals moved between the sectors, starting new programs in existing NGOs, establishing new organizations, and transforming skills, methods, and outlooks. Deeper and sometimes contentious contact between NGOs in the poor countries and those based in the rich, industrial countries exposed international NGOs from both fields to the often seamless multiple identities and strategies of the social movements and local NGOs. International NGOs, particularly in human rights, felt pressure from southern NGOs and movements to take up the long-neglected ESC rights agenda. Mutual contact with organizations in the indigenous peoples', labor, environmental, and especially global women's movements was often a key factor in establishing relationships.

By tracing the involvement of activists in international human rights, development, and other fields in local and global episodes, we demonstrate an increasing intensity of engagement between the methods and cultures of human rights and those of development. Human rights–based rhetoric, analysis, and demands grew more frequent and influential in formal settings such as the position documents and shadow statements of NGOs at global conferences, as well as in the less formal statements and demands of participants in local conflicts over projects. These experiences of the 1980s and early 1990s formed the social, political, and organizational bases for the current convergence of human rights, development, and environmental advocacy and new rights strategies they have employed.

At local debates and conflicts over large-scale infrastructure projects, community organizations, NGOs, and social movements advanced strategies that combined human rights, development, and environmental themes. Intense conflicts, such as those around the World Bank–financed Narmada dam projects in western India, brought environmental and indigenous rights advocates together and united development, environmental, and human rights NGOs (Khagram 2004). Many of these volatile cases involved the World Bank, its private sector lending arm the International Finance Corporation (IFC), and multinational corporations, compelling human rights advocates to seek out and learn from the experience of development and environment advocates in lobbying the World Bank.

These high-profile episodes had immediate results for the international NGOs that became involved. They participated in new networks, encountered cross-sector analysis of issues, developed common goals, and shared strategies, especially for the challenges of influencing the multinational corporations. As we demonstrate in chapter 4, over the course of the 1990s these networks' goals converged around agendas that crossed sector lines: (a) the right to information about planned projects, (b) the right of affected communities to consultation, (c) protection of the rights and safety of community leaders and activists, and (d) the defense of housing and water rights of communities relocated by projects.

In the global arena UN-sponsored global conferences brought diverse NGOs and social movement organizations together at a series of United Nations Conferences on the Environment and Development (Rio de Janeiro 1992), Human Rights (Vienna 1992), the World Summit on Social Development (Copenhagen 1995), and the Fourth World Conference on Women (Beijing 1995). These global conferences directly contributed to the development of new rights advocacy for NGOs, as they formed alliances, developed common strategies, shared information, and learned new methods for litigation and policy advocacy. The fora also deepened northern NGOs' exposure to southern NGOs, some of which had worked more seamlessly at the nexus of human rights and development for a decade or more.

In these local and global interactions, crosscutting social movements demonstrated the potential of integrating human rights standards, human rights advocacy methods, and an agenda for social change. The global women's movement, indigenous rights movement, and other social movement organizations and networks provided a foundation for integration of development, environmental, and human rights approaches, and gave evidence of the potential influence of global movements.

Through these developments activists, practitioners, and organizations operating at the international level came into sustained contact with each other across sector lines. Demands and incentives grew for individual NGOs to innovate, form alliances, and even create new organizational hybrids. Individuals moved among the organizations and across sector lines, further deepening the exchange. Together, these experiences impelled some individuals and organizations into work at the nexus of development and human rights and forced them to accommodate to new trends and new constituencies, shift the focus of their advocacy and research agendas, and ultimately expand their missions and active agendas.

Implications of the New Rights Advocacy

These trends in human rights and development are significant in themselves, but they have broader implications for larger theoretical and policy issues regarding NGOs as political and strategic actors; power, social movements, and the nature of human rights; and the changing nature of accountability for human rights. We will revisit these four issues in the chapters that follow, as they spell out some of the larger implications of the trends in human rights and development.

IMPLICATIONS FOR NGOs MANAGING CHANGE

Two disciplinary approaches to NGOs, grounded in international relations and in organizational management, seldom address each other directly. But they offer contrasting views of international NGOs, on the one hand as political actors driven by principle, or on the other hand as organizations seeking strategic advantage in competitive environments. Power is a central feature in our analysis of each of the sectors, but power and the political agendas of the NGO actors are not the only dimensions of NGOs' strategic choices. NGOs and their fields cannot be fully understood if they are treated only as political actors.

The heroic view of international NGOs is represented by Keck and Sikkink's (1998) argument that transnational issue networks are principled and values-driven networks of individuals and organizations. A dozen titles from the past ten years—such as *The Conscience of the UN, Making a Better World, Will Civil Society Save the World?, Restructuring World Politics, Diplomacy of Conscience, Global Citizen Action*—have also advanced this view. We discuss the strategies and models they employ below; for the present, international relations theorists have tended to see NGOs, usually sympathetically, as political actors.

NGO management scholars and practitioners have taken a variety of approaches to the problems that arise for a voluntary organization operating transnationally: resource constraints (Fowler 2000b), interorganizational partnerships (Fowler 2000a), transnational NGO "families" (Lindenberg and Bryant 2001). All these emphasize the adoption of solutions that permit NGOs to accomplish programmatic and sometimes policy agendas. Institutionalist approaches (Ostrom 1990) similarly emphasize the fit of organizational forms to the social and development needs of a society or community.

Sociological theories of organizations suggest a variety of ways to understand organizations, change, and resistance to change. Since the 1960s, organizational theories have emphasized organizations' tendency to protect themselves from uncertainties in their working environment (Thompson 1967; Pfeffer and Salancik 1978), the role of cultural expectations about organizations in forming the standards, myths, and rituals to which organizations tend to conform (Dimaggio and Powell 1983), population ecology approaches (Hannan and Freedman 1989), and others.

Our approach treats NGOs both as political actors and as organizations in a competitive environment with demanding constituencies, influenced by changes in international power relations both through those changes' effects on NGOs' principled political agendas and through the pressures these changes place on NGOs as organizations. Principled organizations are organizations nonetheless, and they are affected by the demands of competitive sectors as well as by the demands of growing inequality and need. But the fact that these organizational imperatives exist does not render NGOs' principles inauthentic or ephemeral. What is important is to examine the organizational change process closely and understand how principled considerations and organizational factors interact to produce the decisions that emerge.

Implementing changes in NGO programs requires organizational change, and implementing deep changes in methodology or mission may require fundamental organizational transformation. We trace internal processes of organizational change in detail (chapters 2 and

3) and observe the roles of key organizations and of key individuals in fomenting sector-wide change, forging intersector alliances, and creating new hybrid organizational forms (chapter 4).

Changes among NGOs manifest themselves in organizational strategies that affect allocation of resources among different existing aspects of their operational work, at a rhetorical or tactical level (in particular campaigns or programs) and through methodological change, which challenges core operating principles and can lead to an organizational transformation. All these levels of change are significant to practitioners in the field, but change in methodology is the most complex and most in need of explanation.

We use "methodology" to refer to organizations' standard operating procedures, their principal means of implementing their missions. Methodologies are not easily or quickly changed, because unlike political tactics or choices of priorities among several strategies, methodologies depend upon NGOs' structure, skill base, image, and capacities. Profound shifts of this kind occur only under unusual pressure or in response to powerful incentives, because they involve changes in the basic method of operation that are often at the core of an organization's identity.

Among the principal NGO actors in the chapters that follow, Human Rights Watch, Amnesty International, CARE, and Oxfam have identifiable methodologies that strongly shape their response to pressures and policy changes.

Human Rights Watch forms its agenda around its strong capacity for investigating and reporting on human rights violations. A choice to adopt a new program area, such as women's human rights or human rights and HIV/AIDS, is a strategic choice, a response to changes in the environment, and it is conditioned by Human Rights Watch's methodology, which rests heavily on investigation and reporting. This is a strategic choice that limits change in the agenda by holding the methodology constant. More specific choices regarding tactics (e.g., which country to investigate) are shaped as well by the fit with Human Rights Watch's investigative and reporting apparatus.

Oxfam outlines a two-pronged organizational methodology. Partnerships with local and national progressive organizations—to finance projects and programs, build organizational capacity, and carry out advocacy—are coupled with international advocacy on global-level issues such as World Bank reform, WTO and trade agreements, debt relief, and HIV/AIDS. Oxfam's redefinition of its mission in terms of five central rights—adoption of a "rights-based" approach—reshapes the methodology by insisting that priority issues be identified by reference to unfulfilled rights, by refocusing partnerships on organizations that promote human rights, and by giving attention to specific corporate actors, but it does not fundamentally change the methodology of a development NGO already working through partnerships and emphasizing advocacy.

CARE is likely to experience a more fundamental change in methodology. It has operated with a methodology that involves directly operated CARE-managed development projects and relief operations, with minimal advocacy work. Its adoption of a rights-based approach is a strategic choice that the senior staff is interpreting as requiring a reorientation of organizational priorities, an increase in public advocacy work, and a shift toward partnerships in its projects. How a rights-based approach is to be integrated with CARE's Household Livelihood Survey and other core parts of its antipoverty analysis and planning is central to the NGO's debates in chapter 3.

Amnesty International's approach to implementing its ESC rights agenda contrasts with that of Human Rights Watch. Amnesty International is prepared to open the question of methodology as it begins to act on the full spectrum of human rights. Amnesty International's distinctive methodology, mobilizing its volunteer membership to write letters and take other actions in response to individual cases of human rights abuse (torture, arbitrary detention), may require some adaptation to be applied to the health rights of people infected with the HIV virus or the land rights of Zimbabweans expelled from their farms, while it retains it historical approach of mobilizing its grass-roots membership.

For both sectors, we need a means of analyzing and comparing observed organizational changes to make reliable judgments about whether deep organizational changes are under way or an NGO is taking less significant steps to appear to conform to sector norms.

We draw on theories of organizational change and an analysis of the significance of human rights guarantees for NGO methods and agenda to identify organizational changes that constitute "discontinuous" or "strategic" change in organizational direction and methodology, as opposed to "incremental" (Nadler and Tushman 1995). Two sets of organizational theory provide a workable and consistent answer. Structural contingency theory focuses on the organization's need to minimize uncertainty in its environment and protect standard operations that are the core of its work. Sociologist James Thompson (1967) showed that every organization copes with a "task environment," which is the principal source of uncertainty and principal threat to its organizational performance and control.

Pfeffer and Salancik (1978, 24, 34) argue that perturbations from the environment are central for understanding organizations' behavior. Organizations weigh and balance competing demands and bids for influence and control, and coping with these demands drives much of any organization's behavior. The key to coping with uncertainty is protecting the organization's "core technology," its machines, skills, knowledge, training, strategies, procedures, and special characteristics of inputs and outputs (Scott 1985).

The payoffs for research—the analytical benefits of integrating organizational and political approaches—are threefold. They allow for a fuller understanding of NGOs themselves, they permit human rights advocates to make a realistic assessment of the difficulties of bringing ESC rights into the mainstream of human rights advocacy, and they provide a basis for a skeptical interpretation of the development NGOs' embrace of rights-based approaches, an interpretation that neither naively accepts their claims nor lapses into cynicism about the potential for any independent principled choices by development agencies.

IMPLICATIONS FOR UNDERSTANDING THE POWER OF NGOs AND SOCIAL MOVEMENTS

Power is central to this analysis. Understanding the different ways development and human rights practitioners talk and think about power, and the relationships between social movements' power claims and economic and social rights, requires a conceptual framework that recognizes the various forms power takes. The forms of power that are of interest in contemporary NGO practice include NGOs' capacity to influence state policy and behavior, but they also extend to their ability to influence corporate behavior, the activities of international financial institutions and the trade regime (drawing on environmental NGOs' work), and their success in expanding the popular understanding and embrace of the full range of human rights standards (drawing on development and social movement thinking.)

Power, then, is broader than the realist notion of contesting interests among states. Barnett and Duvall's (2005) definition, following Scott (2001), encompasses relations among nonstate actors and focuses attention on certain effects of social relations. Power is "the production, in and through social relations, of effects that shape the capacities of actors to determine their circumstances and fate." "Actors" here is deliberately broad; power may be exercised through legislation that restricts a government agency's power, through governments' actions that set the direction of an international organization, through an organized consumer campaign that makes a marketplace strategy untenable for a corporation or industry, or through the decision of a landlord to evict tenant farmers. Barnett and Duvall's approach allows for the variety of forms that power can take. In addition to the direct exercise of compulsory power by one actor over the behavior of another, power may be exercised through institutions and their rules and by shaping or even defining the interests and capabilities of other actors.

NGOs have adopted a variety of postures toward power. Social movements and advocacy campaigns on economic policy issues often directly challenge power holders in corporations and major governments, and international human rights NGOs have continuously worked to increase the power and legitimacy of international standards, while also empowering those who wield rights claims against the duty holders. But development organizations are less explicit in their posture toward power and have largely embraced a discourse and practice that emphasizes capacity building, public participation, and often vague language about empowerment of communities. Thus power and its misuse by state or nonstate actors has not generally been the direct target of development work, nor has this work directly focused on increasing the power of communities to challenge powerful institutions.

James Ferguson's (1990) argument, that "development" is an "antipolitics machine" that renders the politics of social development into a matter of allegedly apolitical expertise and bureaucratic power, portrays a development unconcerned with democratic institutions and accomplished at covering over the power relations that pervade development. Development in general became more able to enter into the discourse of political institutions in the 1990s, but there remains a strong tendency to shy away from discussing power relations. While some NGOs acknowledge the conflictive politics of development and embrace a struggle for power over economic resources and social policy, the sector as a whole has been more concerned with building the legitimacy of its central project of cooperative development. Indeed, development NGOs and humanitarian agencies have unwittingly been caught up in the exercise of power by the United States and other governments when they practice neutral humanitarianism in their emergency relief and community development work. We take up this subject in chapter 3.

Human rights organizations themselves also address power indirectly. Power is not prominent in the lexicon of the major international human rights NGOs, but it surfaces with reference to increasing the power, legitimacy, or authority of the human rights standards, legitimacy that is linked, in turn, to checking the unrestricted power of human rights–violating governments (Risse, Ropp, and Sikkink 1999). International NGOs seldom directly assert power for themselves as an organization or sector, at least explicitly, yet they often target powerful governments as leverage to impact third-party governments directly responsible for violating human rights.

But there is an important tradition of human rights thought that argues that human rights are much more deeply steeped in power and in conflicts over power. Stammers, for example, sees human rights claims as arising out of social movements and their efforts to increase their own power or circumscribe the powers of others. These assertions of power, he argues, are the keys to understanding human rights, not any pre-existent right inherent in the order of nature, nor their standing in international treaties, covenants, and conventions (Stammers 1999). This understanding of power is closely tied to our understanding of new rights advocacy.

Social movements and community organizations, with whom the international NGOs increasingly work in the context of new rights advocacy, are usually not hesitant to assert—or defy—power, and an important point of comparison among development NGOs, human rights NGOs, and the networks and alliances they associate with is their sharply differing postures with respect to power. Social movements' direct and forthright challenges to state power and to powerful social institutions have contributed to the uneasy relations between international NGOs—especially in development—and social movements. The 1999 Seattle WTO protests laid bare the chasm that divided "antiglobalization" movements, as they were then called, from even the most progressive among the mainstream international development NGOs, Oxfam (Nelson 2002; Bendana 2004; Scholte 2004).

The difficulty for international NGOs lies in part in their ambiguous position, sometimes able to win a place at the table for dialogue with the World Bank or the G-8 governments, yet eager to retain the legitimacy that comes with being affiliated with mass movements. We review several cases that suggest that the language of human rights can serve as the political and conceptual bridge between some movements and activist NGOs, in both human rights and development.

Finally, the new rights advocacy is shaping social movement approaches to globalization. Popular movements against globalization are increasingly attempting to apply the full range of human rights standards to economic, trade, and financial policy issues and to the regulation of corporate behavior. Underlying an array of popular movements since the 1990s is a growing embrace by activists of human rights concepts and strategies as standards for policy and behavior of economic actors and standards for some form of effective international regulation. This process of building the authority of human rights standards in economic and social issues parallels the assertion of civil and political rights as standards for governments by earlier movements against torture, disappearances, and denial of civil rights. New rights advocacy incorporates civil and political rights guarantees for those demanding a right to participate in critical economic policy forums and development decisions.

New rights advocacy calls more serious attention to ESC rights in national and international policymaking. These rights, which are legally and theoretically coequal with civil and political guarantees such as freedom of speech and protections against arbitrary detention and torture, have not developed the same support among powerful industrial countries, nor among NGO advocates, that civil and political human rights now enjoy. The new rights advocacy challenges the relative obscurity of ESC rights and calls for reintegration with civil and political rights.

IMPLICATIONS FOR HUMAN RIGHTS BEYOND
THE VIOLATING STATE

What now attracts NGOs to the new rights advocacy is the potential of human rights standards and methodologies to transform international policy advocacy. Development grounded in internationally recognized rights and obligations—not simply in needs and generosity—places explicit obligations on governments in both the poor and wealthy countries, and on international agencies. Human rights standards create bases for accountability of NGOs themselves and of corporations and governments. The development field has gone through many fashions in doctrine and practice, but none represents such a profound shift in orientation as the new human rights–based approaches to development practice.

Likewise, the new economic and social rights advocacy of traditional human rights NGOs allows them to address the root causes of civil and political rights violations while targeting economic actors and the dramatic economic changes of the past decade. This broadening of mission is also fundamentally transforming the historic human rights sector. The new rights advocacy includes multiple trends with diverse historical roots and implications.

The new rights advocacy entails a fundamentally new understanding of accountability for the failure to meet human rights standards. In traditional civil and political rights advocacy, governments are accused of practicing arbitrary detention, torture, or discriminatory access to legal remedies, and international actors are persuaded to exert leverage, pressing the offending governments to amend policies and practices. New rights advocacy is not constrained by the sole focus on the state as duty bearer and violator of human rights. It targets many institutions, including international financial institutions, transnational corporations, trade regimes, rich-country governments and poor-country governments themselves, whose policies and behavior have an impact on economic and social rights and/or civil and political rights in poor countries. Advocates question the authority of international agencies and rules that weaken states' capacity to meet their obligations associated with social and economic rights. They also call on rich countries to provide more generous and effective development assistance, invoking the provision in Article 2 of the ICESCR that establishes international coresponsibility and cooperation to meet ESC rights (Jochnick 1999). The effects of broadening its advocacy "targets" vary from case to case, as we will see.

These changes in NGOs' practice across the sectors challenge current models of how NGOs influence policy. Scholars have tended to assess NGOs' efficacy as political actors in terms of their ability to influence state behavior, a focus that grew out of scholarship influenced by civil and political rights advocacy and the disciplinary subfield in which the debate has taken place, international relations. The study of NGOs and of networks in which they participate gained legitimacy in international relations (particularly in Keck and Sikkink's influential work) by demonstrating NGOs' relevance to state conduct. But the realities of NGO work at the human rights–development nexus call for a less state-centric approach, drawing on social movement theory and broader conceptions of power, and taking into account the growing understanding of corporate influence in the international political economy.

IMPLICATIONS FOR THE DEVELOPMENT PARADIGM

The new rights advocacy is the first fundamental challenge to a market-dominated development framework that reshaped national economies and international trade and finance during the 1980s and 1990s. New movements are drawing on human rights standards to challenge the application of market logic to the delivery of water and basic services, to argue for the right to agrarian reform and education, and to assert the primacy of human health considerations in setting national and international policy regarding HIV/AIDS. Resistance to privatization and liberalization plans has been a feature of national politics in developing countries at least since the 1970s. New rights advocacy movements are challenging market-driven orthodoxy at the international institutions with greater political force and legitimacy than critics of structural adjustment policies have previously mustered.

Tracking the Origins

As we turn in chapters 2 and 3 to the two fields—first human rights, then development—we investigate whether and how international NGOs are adopting new strategic postures and methods for advancing human rights and development, and what effects these changes have on the organizations and the broader fields.

We will observe important parallels and symmetries in the changes, limitations, and resistance to change across the sectors. But there are also important differences among major international NGOs in the fields and between the two fields. International NGOs in the two fields were affected differently by major political trends in the 1980s and 1990s, their embrace of ESC rights has a different organizational significance, and they are affected differently by some of the factors that have long led to the secondary status of ESC rights in the human rights field.

They begin in very different positions with respect to ESC rights. For international development NGOs, the turn to human rights, and to ESC rights in particular, constitutes a potential paradigm shift, a reorientation that embraces the international legal and moral framework of human rights as a new kind of ethical and operational guide for development practice. For human rights NGOs, the shift has a different meaning. Mainstream international human rights NGOs find themselves in the position of turning toward the second of the twin covenants that codify human rights principles, reintegrating through their active agendas the two halves of the human rights legal corpus after de-emphasizing and largely neglecting economic and social rights throughout a generation of promotion of civil and political human rights.

This effort to reintegrate and reorient the fields will not be easy. Fulfilling social rights is costly, and although countries and major subnational regions such as the Indian state of Kerala have achieved remarkable health and education outcomes on modest budgets, in general budget constraints present barriers that are much less troublesome for civil and political rights. The principle articulated in Article 2 of the ICESCR, that international actors share the responsibility in some measure through a variety of means including "providing assistance," is yet to be fully operationalized, and any extensive obligations are sure to encounter resistance. International NGO activists in both fields also recognize that the international obligations articulated in Article 2 will extend beyond providing development assistance to shaping the rules of the global economy in ways that make it possible for governments to meet the full range of their human rights obligations.

The partial and sometimes tentative embrace of new rights advocacy by the leading international NGOs in the two fields, then, offers a study in the differences and adaptations driven by both political and organizational factors. But it is also the story of a kind of convergence between two historic fields that is reshaping both while also reshaping the relations among NGOs in the global North and South, social movements, and rich- and poor-country governments.

2

TRANSFORMING
THE HUMAN RIGHTS MOVEMENT
Human Rights NGOs Embrace
ESC Rights

*I*n recent years Amnesty International has broadened its mission in recognition that there are many more prisoners of poverty than prisoners of conscience, and that millions endure the torture of hunger and slow death from preventable disease. Given the interconnected nature of all human rights violations, engaging with economic, social, and cultural rights has enabled Amnesty International to address complex human rights problems in a more holistic and comprehensive manner.

—Human Rights and Human Dignity: A Primer on Economic, Social and Cultural Rights, Amnesty International, 2005

The Emerging Movement for ESC Rights

Over the past decade, advocacy for economic and social rights has grown more widespread, more often internationally sanctioned, and at times more effective. This advocacy, wrapped within the internationally recognized standards of human rights, is expanding as organizations promoting economic and social policies through the international human rights framework grow, attract support from grassroots and international NGOs, and help to shape and expand national and transnational NGO networks.

United Nations agencies and other international agencies have taken steps to assist in developing more rigorous definition, monitoring, and implementation of ESC rights. The UN Commission on Human Rights appointed special rapporteurs on education, food, housing, and highest attainable standard of health. At key UN bodies from the UNDP to the World Health Organization and Food and Agricultural Organization, rights-based approaches proliferated, reinforcing the move by UN human rights bodies to focus on economic and social rights and lending legitimacy and support to similar steps among NGOs.

The growth in ESC rights advocacy, and with it the transformation of the human rights movement, encompasses two processes: the development of new movements and organizations that explicitly link critical human needs issues to social and economic rights standards; and the expansion of mandates by traditional civil and political rights groups to cover ESC rights.

While new organizations and networks are forming to promote ESC rights, traditional international human rights groups are grappling with adoption of a "full spectrum" approach to human rights advocacy, promoting the entire range of human rights principles and standards embodied in the Universal Declaration of Human Rights (UDHR) and the two binding international treaties that were developed to legally codify the UDHR. As examples, Human Rights Watch (HRW) and others have adopted some ESC rights analysis and advocacy, while Amnesty International's international policymaking body took a decisive step in 2001 toward full engagement with ESC rights.

This chapter first examines the international conditions that have changed over the last two decades and how traditional civil and political human rights organizations have altered their strategies in response, leading to the eventual embrace of economic and social rights advocacy. Second, three case studies of traditional international human rights organizations, and of the new organizations that have emerged that focus explicitly on ESC rights, allow us to observe the variety of patterns of adoption and organizational change.

Third, we turn to debates within the human rights community about the efficacy of traditional human rights organizations adopting ESC agendas, including questions of ideology, methods, capacity, and organizational priorities and identity. We conclude with some observations about the future challenges of ESC rights advocacy and the growing convergence of human rights groups with development and environmental agencies embracing a rights-based approach to development.

Traditional International Human Rights NGOs and ESC Rights

The cold war dichotomy of civil and political versus social, economic, and cultural rights set the framework for future advocacy on human rights. Most recognized international human rights groups emerged in the West and reflected a bias toward civil and political rights. The early human rights NGOs took on the most egregious forms of human rights violations recognized by Western governments. Thus torture, mistreatment, execution, and denial of due process for political beliefs became the central set of human rights embraced by newly emergent human rights groups. Human rights NGOs also understood that they would be most influential if they focused on issues readily embraced by Western constituencies, allowing activists to build a power base for international advocacy. With the expansion of repressive regimes associated with the Eastern bloc, and the tendency of the United States and other Western countries to treat human rights abuses by allied regimes as tolerable tradeoffs to achieve short-term political stability, the constituency began to grow in the West for civil and political rights protection.

Amnesty International, for example, was founded in 1961 and evolved its methodology for protecting individual civil and political human rights in this cold war environment. Addressing individuals' rights to political freedoms and bodily integrity, Amnesty International garnered international support that transcended ideological differences by targeting human rights violations by totalitarian Soviet bloc governments and abusive regimes in the southern hemisphere while challenging the Western rationale for tacitly or directly supporting repression by anticommunist regimes. Coupling solid research and letter-writing tactics, Amnesty International was quickly recognized for its successes in securing human rights protection and for building an international grassroots movement (Korey 1998). While its mandate evolved over time, its focus remained relatively circumscribed within the larger system of human rights, responding to the many cases of civil and political rights abuses.

Other international human rights NGOs replicated Amnesty's focus on a subset of civil and political rights monitoring and advocacy. While each had a different methodology or constituency, the growth of international NGOs formed in the United States alone, such as International Human Rights Law Group (now Global Rights), Human Rights Watch, and the Lawyers Committee for Human Rights (now Human Rights First), effectively (if unintentionally) reinforced and popularized the idea that human rights were civil and political rights.

But dramatic international system changes forced human rights NGOs to alter strategies. As the cold war system began to unravel and new regimes led by human rights activists or shaped by human rights principles came to power, the optimistic view flourished that a new era for global human rights advocacy had opened. As the world witnessed a decade of democratization in the 1990s and the cold war rationale that had legitimated international support for undemocratic and repressive government was weakened, international human rights NGOs debated how to hold newly independent and democratic regimes to international human rights standards and how to address past rights violations.

But it was a brief period of optimism for human rights advocates. Within a few short years, communal conflicts and carnage in Yugoslavia and Rwanda put the euphoria to rest. The failure of the international community to effectively address these conflicts without the cold war imperative or significant economic interests brought the new era's challenges into stark form, and human rights NGOs grappled with how to respond.

As international conditions changed, human rights and humanitarian crises multiplied, economic globalization began to take hold, and national and transnational social movements in the global South grew in size and sophistication, the operating conditions for international human rights NGOs also changed significantly. The changes compelled a rethinking of strategies and produced patterns in NGO activity that we characterize in the stages sketched below. Each stage ultimately led those organizations toward a focus on ESC rights, produced greater collaboration with the development sector, and addressed more directly the economic "root" causes of civil and political rights violations. Ultimately, these strategic changes led to debates on whether international human rights NGOs should directly embrace research and advocacy on ESC rights, not only as root causes of civil and political rights violations, but as legitimate human rights in themselves.

IMPUNITY AND UNIVERSALITY

By the mid-1990s, human rights NGOs faced four critical factors in the post–cold war international environment that challenged their traditional approaches to work in civil and political human rights. These primary factors—the proliferation of communal conflicts and genocidal conditions, the global explosion of civil society, the affront to universality posed by key governments and reactionary forces, and the declining strength of the United Nations—stimulated the first round of strategic changes. Reaction to these factors led to development of two immediate strategies: the reassertion of the universality of rights through strengthening both the United Nations machinery and the capacity of human rights NGOs in the global South, and a focus on developing norms and institutions of accountability for redress of past human rights violations. These challenges, and some strategic responses by human rights NGOs, are described briefly below.

Communal Conflict and Accountability

The growing number of communal or ethnic conflicts appeared to accelerate with the dismantling of cold war alliance systems. Human rights NGOs, faced with the carnage of Rwanda and the former Yugoslavia, grappled with how to respond to such crises before they reached genocidal proportions and how to ensure that the post-conflict era would not spiral back into patterns of violence.

The response of human rights groups in the early 1990s was multifaceted. They stepped up advocacy for mechanisms of accountability for mass violations of human rights and genocide, from truth commissions to internationalized war crimes tribunals to ultimately an International Criminal Court; began efforts to hold nonstate actors (insurgent groups in civil conflicts) accountable to international human rights standards in conflict situations; and focused on developing early warning and crises response systems to enable rapid, effective action in the face of genocidal conditions. Human rights advocates called for greater attention to "root causes" of communal conflicts and developed initiatives to pursue diverse strategies to track patterns of identity-based discrimination by governments, to counter the public incitement to mass hatred through media and education, and to control the instruments of war, such as the small arms trade and the use of child soldiers.

Global Civil Society

By the early 1990s the growth of local, national, and regional NGOs throughout the world meant that international human rights NGOs now had new partners at the local and national levels to document human rights abuses, partners who challenged what were often forty-year-old methods and operating procedures of the international groups. Globalization was not limited to the rapid advance of capital mobility and near-universal embrace of neoliberal economic policies, it also meant the globalization of communication systems and sharing of strategies between geographically dispersed social movements and NGOs. Globalization played a critical role in changing relations between international NGOs and their counterparts in the poor countries.

In response to these changes in global civil society, the international groups began to focus on institution and capacity building at the local level, training and assisting southern or eastern NGOs to conduct investigations of human rights, litigate cases, and develop campaigning tools. They worked to protect the rights of local human rights defenders, a strategy (described below) that took on more significance as international NGOs grappled with economic globalization later in the decade.

Universality and the Erosion of the UN Human Rights Machinery

The 1993 World Conference on Human Rights in Vienna was expected by some to be a celebration of the post–cold war era, the new freedom of the United Nations to operate in a less politicized international environment, and NGO human rights successes. Instead it marked a watershed moment for the integrity of the human rights system, as NGOs battled a coalition of governments determined to undermine the principle of the universality of human rights standards and weaken the UN human rights system. Led in part by women's human rights groups, the conference ended with a weak but successful renewal of support for the concepts of universality, indivisibility, and interdependence of rights with some key, specific commitments to strengthening the UN machinery (Dorsey 1996).

The challenge to shore up the fundamental concept of universality of rights was compounded by shifts in the foreign policy priorities of Western governments. A new Democratic administration in the United States made promoting free-market democracies, rather than human rights, its top priority, resulting in human rights regressions, including the delinking of trade and aid from human rights guarantees (Mann 1999). Human rights advocates battled throughout the early to mid-1990s for attention to human rights in the post–cold war economic policies of the most powerful governments on the international stage.

CONFRONTING ECONOMIC GLOBALIZATION

The focus on root causes and early warning for large-scale human rights violations and the reassertion of the universality of rights coincided with a period of rapid economic globalization, which marked a new stage in strategic adaptation for traditional human rights groups. This is not the place for a sustained analysis of the impact of economic globalization on human rights; instead we turn to a brief overview of the stages of strategic response international human rights groups adopted to address those conditions.

For human rights groups, the immediate challenges posed by economic globalization were threefold: how to measure the impact of economic globalization through human rights standards, how to apply international human rights standards to economic actors, and how to remain relevant in the eyes of the emerging NGO and social movement mobilizations opposing corporate globalization.

Most large international human rights organizations, historically state-focused, had limited experience in monitoring corporations or international financial institutions or targeting them for grassroots campaigns. There was growing attention to corporate accountability issues, and international human rights NGOs intervened in select issues with the International Monetary Fund or the World Bank, calling for policies that conformed to human rights standards and for human rights impact assessments of loans. But international NGOs' grassroots campaigning remained largely targeted on governments, a focus that only began to change by the mid 1990s, as the case studies that follow demonstrate.

Additionally, the "decade of despair" (UNDP 2000) left traditional international human rights NGOs vulnerable to the challenge that their work was not relevant to the 1.2 billion people living in abject poverty, heightened inequality, and social marginalization. With the explosion of southern NGOs and ESC rights–oriented groups and their focus on economic actors and on the impact of development policies, traditional human rights groups increasingly came under fire for (at best) adopting an inadequate approach to human rights advocacy and (at worst) for blocking the full potential of the human rights framework to promote the rights of peoples hardest hit by economic globalization. As international exchanges of perspectives intensified and began to change the power dynamics among NGOs, international human rights activists increasingly recognized the centrality of ESC rights to impoverished peoples' lives.[1] Criticisms from smaller NGOs and southern NGOs were not new, but increasingly the large, traditional international human rights NGOs began to implement new ways to respond to the calls for a human rights approach to social and economic conditions.

RESPONDING TO THE CALL FOR ADVOCACY ON ESC RIGHTS

The field of human rights was already dramatically changing. With the advance of new strategies to react to international system changes and the growth in new human rights actors, the changed strategic orientations of international human rights NGOs—historically focused on targeting state violations of civil and political rights—presented profound changes for organizational management and constituency education. Supporters of human rights such as Amnesty International had to be educated about new human rights crises and trained in new strategies. Media and public education would also necessarily follow. In the period of one decade, assumptions on which the previous thirty years of advocacy were built were undergoing radical reorientation.

The rapid development of new organizations working on human rights, the intensified interaction with the development and environment fields, and the growing call by social movements for international human rights groups to address economic actors and economic and social policies created internal demands for changes in strategic priorities and, in some cases, methods of operation.

Defending the Defenders of Human Rights

"Defending the defenders" initiatives seek to protect those trade, development, women's, and environmental activists who defend human rights in their own countries and whose own civil and political rights are often violated as they protest labor conditions or the impact of development projects. Focusing on civil and political rights violations of individuals and inspiring worldwide action on cases with a human face, campaigning on behalf of human rights defenders was a high priority for many human rights organizations from the middle to late 1990s. By creating a "safe" political space and calling international attention to emerging movements and NGOs operating in the global South, the defenders approach has been a critical bridge to building coalitions with NGOs in the development, labor, and environmental movements. It has also reflected a shift in roles and power relations between NGOs based in the West and North and those in the global South.

Action on ESC Rights

In the late 1980s and early 1990s, many international human rights groups began incorporating analysis of the relationship of civil and political rights to economic and social rights. Many had a history of basic public education on all human rights, despite a more narrow focus in their direct advocacy. But by the late 1990s, human rights NGOs began to move from talking about ESC rights and the principles of indivisibility and interdependence in their reports and public education programs to linking them to their advocacy agendas. In this period, the gradual appearance of analysis around ESC and interdependence was converted into rapid adoption of new approaches. As we argue in chapter 1, new advocacy on ESC rights reflected both external and internal pressures for change. International human rights NGOs perceived that to be both effective in addressing a changed world and legitimate in the eyes of their counterparts in the poor countries, they had to lend greater credibility to economic and social rights.

How did the international human rights NGOs incorporate new agendas on ESC rights? The answer varies by organization, depending upon leadership, expectation, availability of funds, and pre-existing method of operation, as the following case studies demonstrate.

ORGANIZATIONAL CHANGE IN INTERNATIONAL HUMAN RIGHTS NGOs

By the mid-1990s, international human rights NGOs had already begun to take steps toward new research and advocacy on ESC rights. Some of the most recognized human rights groups, like Human Rights Watch and Amnesty International, were watched carefully by other NGOs. Advocates of ESC rights saw the legitimating potential of such moves, but were concerned that the international NGOs would further bifurcate ESC rights and civil and political rights into a new type of hierarchy. ESC rights advocates were also concerned that the international NGOs would enter this arena not as partners but would dominate, overshadowing decades of work done by smaller NGOs and drawing resources away from those groups already struggling to garner support for the long-marginalized ESC rights agenda.

Others were concerned about the impact on the international NGOs themselves. Would they stretch scarce resources too far to be effective? Would they lose historic constituencies and donor support, or become indistinguishable from other human rights and development groups? Did they have the capacity to manage the change? And is it being sustained?

Three case studies offer insight into how staff members and supporters navigated these debates, and on how organizations manage change and develop new strategies and methods to respond to new conditions. We will look briefly at Human Rights First (formerly Lawyers Committee for Human Rights) and Human Rights Watch, then examine in greater detail change at Amnesty International, given its prominence in the international human rights movement and the complexities of change for its international structure and membership. These are by no means the only international human rights NGOs that have adopted an ESC rights agenda, but their contrasting cases provide important data for tracking changes in the sector.

These three organizations can be seen as representing three different levels of change: (a) program level engagement, (b) limited adoption, and (c) full embrace. Each of the case studies addresses three questions: What reasons do the organizations provide for their new and expanded focus on ESC rights? How has the change manifested itself in research and advocacy, changes in staff or structure, methods, or programmatic focus? How is ESC work integrated into the international NGOs' agendas?

Program Level Engagement

Founded in 1978 in the United States, the Lawyers Committee for Human Rights evolved at a time when the U.S. government supported right-wing dictatorships notorious for civil and political rights abuses. Its adoption of ESC rights was gradual.

In 2003 its stated mission was to "create a secure and humane world by advancing justice, human dignity, and respect for the rule of law . . . support human rights activists . . . protect refugees in flight from persecution and repression; promote fair economic practices by creating safeguards for workers' rights; and help to build a strong international system of justice and accountability for the worst human rights crimes." This statement reflected both the strategic priorities of the organization and its evolution: defending human rights activists, working toward international justice to confront impunity, and a strong focus on labor and immigrant rights.

By 2004, although it had changed its name to "Human Rights First" and amended its mission statement and stated priorities, its work on ESC rights was not reflected in either. In the revised statement, Human Rights First:

- "believes that building respect for human rights and the rule of law will help ensure the dignity to which every individual is entitled and will stem tyranny, extremism, intolerance, and violence . . .

- protects people at risk: refugees who flee persecution, victims of crimes against humanity or other mass human rights violations, victims of discrimination, those whose rights are eroded in the name of national security, and human rights advocates. . . . These groups are often the first victims of societal instability and breakdown; their treatment is a harbinger of wider-scale repression.

- works to prevent violations against these groups and to seek justice and accountability for violations against them."

Human Rights First (HRF) embraced ESC rights gradually and strategically, largely out of its work with workers' rights, corporate accountability, and refugee rights. Under the longtime leadership of Michael Posner, Human Rights First's programs grew and changed to reflect changes in political and economic conditions. In the 1980s, as Lawyers Committee for Human Rights, HRF understood that while governments continued to be a target for human rights monitoring and advocacy, nonstate actors were complicit in human rights violations. HRF became a leader in promoting workers' rights as internationally sanctioned human rights and in developing an advocacy agenda to hold corporations accountable to abuses of labor rights. HRF helped found the Fair Labor Association and the FLA-NGO Advisory Council, which outline and monitor minimum standards for corporations working in developing countries. HRF's Worker's Rights Program also works with other NGOs to monitor practices of textile and garment companies. From its work on corporate complicity in violations of civil and political rights, HRF began to focus on the failure of states to act on a wider array of human rights issues, including the rights to food, water, and safe working conditions.

HRF's program on refuges also helped propel the organization into greater advocacy on ESC rights. According to the director of HRF's International Refugees Program, in emergencies involving massive refugee movements, along with significant concern for individuals' physical integrity, food security, the right to clean water, and access to basic standards of health care surface as top priorities. In refugee crises, these rights are critical to survival but frequently denied, and historic international approaches to humanitarian relief have been increasingly criticized as reactive.[2] As refugee activists sought durable solutions to refugee and humanitarian disasters, they began to turn to human rights approaches, and HRF focused its refugee work on devising long-term solutions with a rights-based focus.

Working with the West African Non Governmental Organizations Refugees and Internally Displaced Network (WARIPNET), HRF developed a set of recommendations for treatment of refugees. The right to food, health, and education became focal points in the joint HRF and WARIPNET report, which identified a wide range of human rights violations against refugees and highlighted their complex and interdependent nature. *From Response to Solution—Strengthening the Protection of Refugees in West Africa* identifies recommendations for national, regional, and UN bodies to protect the ESC rights of refugees. Neglect of the right to health is linked to the systematic denial of other ESC rights and to civil and political human rights violations; investigations in rural Mali documented "as many as eight deaths" among ninety-four women whose sexually transmitted infections were left untreated due to "delays and inadequacies in the delivery of health care" (27).

To fully address the human rights violations occurring in response to refugee crises or in refugee camps, HRF and its local partners identified a range of ESC rights recommendations for local governments. Once its analysis is disseminated, HRF provides legal training and educational workshops, working with local NGOs to take steps toward achieving the recommendations. In 2000, WARIPNET invited HRF to conduct a one-week ESC rights workshop for local activists.

At HRF, the decision to adopt an emphasis on ESC rights was not controversial, but evolutionary. Work on labor rights and the sweatshop campaigns reflected the interdependence of rights and made the transition for the organization a relatively easy one. And partnerships with local grassroots and national human rights NGOs in their target countries allowed HRF to work collaboratively to develop an effective set of ESC rights recommendations. Many of the ESC rights focal points emerged out of these partnerships, providing evidence for the changing influence of North-South partnerships on the decision and priorities set by international human rights NGOs.[3]

However, shortly thereafter, in a strategic-planning process that shook up the organization's structure in 2003, HRF decided to cut back on its range of programs in order to focus on what it identified as key areas of civil and political human rights and an expanded attention to U.S. domestic human rights, including torture; arbitrary detention; and other abuses by the United States in the war on terror; nondiscrimination, especially antisemitism; and the organization's long-standing attention to the right of asylum in the United States for refugees fleeing political persecution. In an attempt to recast itself with more public campaigning and less policy think-tank and "grasstops" advocacy, HRF effectively eliminated its economic and social rights work, which had allowed for international coalition building and high-level policy advocacy but had proven hard to mold into campaigns. By 2004, HRF had cut its International Refugees and

Workers Rights programs altogether, and by 2008 it returned to a more traditional human rights agenda. While the organization never adopted ESCR at the mission level, it is unclear whether they will adopt ESCR advocacy in the future. If there is substantial change in U.S. foreign policy, there might be an opening to return to the previous work on workers and refugee rights or direct ESCR advocacy. These changes, though, suggest that the additional resources needed to combat HR abuses in the wake of the war on terror undermined progress towards new ESCR work.

Limited Adoption

In September 1992, Human Rights Watch published "Indivisible Human Rights: The Relationship of Political and Civil Rights to Survival, Subsistence and Poverty." The report's stated objective is to demonstrate how subsistence depends upon the existence of political and civil rights, which takes on the Eastern bloc governments' argument that civil and political rights cannot be enjoyed until basics subsistence has been obtained. It argues that civil and political rights allow people to obtain food, to keep land for subsistence farming, organize for economic advancement, and to resist environmental damage.

The report is significant for three reasons. First, it was released in the run-up to the World Conference on Human Rights, where the concepts of universality and interdependence were being contested. The conference helped motivate traditional international human rights NGOs to signal that they were beginning to redefine their approaches. Although the report is a defense of the focus on civil and political rights, it recognizes an altered operating environment and articulates a sophisticated linkage between issues of economic development and environment.

Second, it reflects the growing influence of southern NGOs and their perspectives and the shift in power relations between international NGOs and their grassroots counterparts. The report begins by quoting the final document of the tenth conference of the Heads of State of Non Aligned Countries, who expressed concern about selectivity in promoting human rights and the tendency to "neglect economic, social and cultural rights which relate more immediately to mankind's needs for food, shelter and health care and for the eradication of poverty and illiteracy."

Third, it demonstrated international NGOs' desire to respond to the growing demands for recognition of ESC and environmental rights by acknowledging them as the "root causes" of civil and political rights violations, demonstrating that the denial of civil and political rights can lead to famine and poverty, and showing how civil and political rights protections create political space for economic, social, and environmental advocacy.

Although this report did not itself represent a shift of focus in research and advocacy, it did signal change. By the mid-1990s, HRW began to argue for a particular approach to ESC rights, applying the tried-and-true methods international human rights NGOs had used successfully for decades in protecting civil and political rights to specific categories of ESC rights violations.

In a widely distributed and hotly debated article published in *Human Rights Quarterly* in 2004, HRW executive director Kenneth Roth articulated his views of the challenges international human rights NGOs would face in adopting ESC rights and of the appropriate focus for organizations historically focused on civil and political rights. Roth embraces the concept of interdependence and argues that there is a place for ESC rights, but cautions that human rights NGOs should confine their work to issues where the violator and remedy can be clearly identified and where the traditional methodology of naming and shaming can be effective. The debate over this article is detailed later in this chapter.

Roth's article is consistent with Human Rights Watch's explicit approach to ESC rights, clearly articulated in its publications web site: "[In addressing ESC rights, w]e focus particularly on situations in which our methodology of investigation and reporting is most effective, such as when arbitrary or discriminatory governmental conduct lies behind an economic, social and cultural rights violation." ESC rights "are an integral part of the body of international human rights law, with the same character and standing as civil and political rights. We conduct research and advocacy on economic, social, and cultural rights using the same methodology that we use with respect to civil and political rights and subject to the same criteria, namely, the ability to identify a rights violation, a violator, and a remedy to address the violation."

How does this approach shape the organization's adoption of issues? A review of HRW reports since 1990 reveals its precision in specifying that a pattern of discrimination is the human rights violation at stake, identifying a clear and typically singular actor as the violator, and delineating a remedy that often requires a change in law or policy, not a reallocation of resources. HRW's methodology is to conduct high-level research on rights violations, often in partnership with allied organizations in target countries, produce reports based upon this documentation, distribute them widely, and conduct intensive media campaigns to promote the remedies they propose. While HRW does some direct advocacy, it does not have a membership base or constituency that may seek to directly influence its policies or strategies.

In the early 1990s there was a strong emphasis on discriminatory policies and the economic and social rights of cultural or ethnic minorities. The first report cited in its catalogue of ESC reports is "Ghana: Official Attacks on Religious Freedom" (1990), which calls on the government to rescind a law requiring all religious bodies to register with the Ministry of the Interior. Other reports in the early and mid-1990s also focus on religious or cultural freedoms in the former Czechoslovakia, Indonesia, Estonia, Pakistan, and Vietnam. With the intensification of conflicts based on religious freedom in the late 1990s, particularly in Sudan, HRW issued a series of reports and intensified its media and advocacy work.

By the late 1990s, government protection of workers' rights had become an important theme for HRW, as they protected workers and labor rights protesters in South Korea and Indonesia and conducted advocacy on free trade agreements. HRW also reported on attacks against leaders of resistance to large-scale development projects and on the forced relocation that often accompanies such projects, as evidenced by reports on the Three Gorges and Narmada dams in China and India.

HRW has dedicated programs for children's and women's rights, and their reports have been used in advocacy efforts by other organizations in the global movement for women's rights. Early reports of the women's rights program, prepared leading up to the Beijing women's conference, linked economic conditions to the abuses of women. "Neither Jobs Nor Justice: State Discrimination against Women in Russia" (Human Rights Watch 1995), for example, cited the impact on women of the worsening economic conditions and in employment discrimination and abuse in the workplace. A series of reports focused on abuses in Mexican _maquiladoras,_ disappearances of women in Mexico and Guatemala, the rights of women and children domestic workers, trafficking of women, and domestic violence issues. HRW has also assigned high priority to the impact of government HIV/AIDS policies on women and children.

Human Rights Watch's program on HIV/AIDS focuses largely on civil and political rights and protecting against discriminatory treatment of HIV/AIDS patients and activists. Applying its established research and documentation strategies, HRW has made the case that discrimination and stigmatization, and sometimes active and systematic violations of the civil and political rights of people living with HIV/AIDS, contribute to their reluctance to seek testing and treatment. Under these circumstances, improved protection of rights against discrimination is a step to improving testing and treatment.

HRW's first reports on human rights and AIDS, in 2001, focused on violence against schoolgirls in South Africa and on HIV/AIDS and children's rights in Kenya. HRW sums up the links between discrimination, human rights abuses, and HIV/AIDS succinctly: human rights abuses "fuel the epidemic," abuses also "follow infection," and research and reporting are needed to protect the rights of vulnerable groups and persons infected with HIV. In addition to reports on this theme, HRW research has also documented limitations placed on AIDS activists in China, intrahousehold inequality and HIV vulnerability in Uganda, and human rights abuse of prisoners and other groups in Russia. In 2005, HRW filed _amicus_ briefs in two cases against USAID, challenging the requirement that NGOs adopt formal policies opposing prostitution as a condition of receiving public health funding from the U.S. overseas aid agency (Human Rights Watch 2005).

Although a review of reports clearly illustrates the consistent pattern of reporting and advocacy on ESC rights employed by HRW, recent reports focus on government programming and its wide impact within the population, as in questions of food security in North Korea, and other reports begin to show creative approaches to the question of recommended remedies for state discrimination in the delivery of economic and social rights, such as the right to education for Iraqi children in Jordan, cited in the box.

IRAQI REFUGEES: THE RIGHT TO EDUCATION

On August 24, 2006, HRW staff member Bill Frelick published an opinion piece in the *Jordan Times* titled "Going to School: A Right Not to Be Ignored." With five hundred thousand Iraqi refugees in Jordan, HRW cited its concern that on the first day of school, tens of thousands of Iraqi children were suffering discrimination and were prevented from attending classes. With crowded classrooms and strained government resources in education and health care, the Jordanian government announced that year that foreign children without residence permits could not attend public schools. Later it reversed its decision, but this produced a confusion that left many children at home, with government administrators, school superintendents, and parents all receiving mixed messages. HRW, acknowledging the financial burden on the government, called on the Jordanian government to ask for international assistance to support Iraqi children's education. HRW also called on the government to change its policy to allow all children to attend school regardless of residency status and to inform their parents, or risk being in violation of the Convention on the Rights of the Child, which guarantees free and compulsory primary education without any discrimination.

HRW's advocacy fits neatly within the organization's prescribed ESC rights boundaries: it details discriminatory practices on the part of a government (clear violation and clear violator), it details a remedy—change the policy and inform parents and schools. But most importantly it does not engage state allocation of resources directly, but indicates that the international community may also be part of the financial solution.

Full Embrace

Amnesty International's (AI) worldwide decision-making body voted in 2001 to give greater attention to ESC rights promotion and to integrate ESC rights with its traditional focus on civil and political rights. Prior to this decision, AI had already committed in 1991 to begin educating about ESC rights. But this step had created a confusing distinction between "promotional" work (education) on ESC rights, and active campaigning, still reserved for civil and political rights. The 2001 decision meant that AI would begin to campaign on some ESC rights that fit within a larger definition of patterns of grave abuses of rights. As such, AI staff and activists would need to rapidly build their skills and understanding of ESC standards, issues, and cases to be effective in applying their methods of research and advocacy to this wider range of human rights issues worldwide. In 2007, AI embraced work on the "full spectrum" of human rights, further clarifying the 2001 decision. What drove these changes and how has AI begun to operationalize this commitment to ESC rights?

By the mid-1990s, AI was working in an integrated way to address the international trends identified above. They were lobbying to support the establishment of the post of a UN high commissioner for human rights, advocating the development of an International Criminal Court (as the ultimate international mechanism to deal with impunity issues), and supporting human rights standards for armed conflict and peacekeeping operations.

As economic change accelerated and as the calls from membership and other human rights advocates grew louder, AI grappled with its own mandate, methodology, and its position on ESC rights. Governed democratically by its international membership, AI has historically been slow to change. Its position on economic sanctions, for example, has been debated for more than a decade, and some policy and mandate debates take on mythological proportion in the lore of AI's staff and membership. Still, two dramatic changes have occurred in the past decade, as AI expanded its focus from state actors to include corporations and other nonstate actors, and adopted a new mission including ESC rights advocacy.

Economic Actors and Corporate Accountability. While the Dutch, British, and U.S. sections of AI took initiatives on economic actors, the commitment to expand work on corporations was movement-wide, signaled by the development of an office on business and human rights in London. Direct corporate involvement in human rights abuses—in cases such as Shell Oil in Nigeria, BP in Colombia, and Freeport MacMahon in Indonesia—provoked quick responses. Strategically, AI used a collaborative approach that coupled an encouragement of corporate best practices with more confrontational demands for accountability in cases where corporate complicity in abuses had been well documented. It increasingly called for corporate codes of conduct and launched its own set of business principles for human rights in the areas of community consultation, security for arrangements, and workplace and labor rights (Amnesty International 2001).

With research teams overburdened in their focus on traditional human rights cases, the data coming out of the research center at the International Secretariat was inconsistent, and larger national sections that can finance their own projects have propelled the ESC rights research forward. In February 2002, the British section of Amnesty International and the International Business Leaders Forum released a major report titled *Business and Human Rights: A Geography of Corporate Risk*. It documents key regional areas of concern and key industries where companies are most vulnerable to the costs and reputational damage associated with human rights violations (Amnesty International United Kingdom and The International Business Leaders Forum 2002). The report reflects AI's continued state-based focus, examining the human rights performance of countries where corporations invest and emphasizing that companies operating in countries with repressive and corrupt regimes risk being drawn into conflict or having their reputations damaged by having human rights violations associated with their operations.

In AI-USA, a new campaign launched in 1998 reflected several of the trends in NGO activity—addressing the root causes of civil and political rights violations, protecting the rights of defenders, monitoring corporate conduct, and building coalitions with development and environmental organizations. The Just Earth! campaign, launched jointly with the Sierra Club to protect the rights of environmental defenders, released a report depicting a larger global pattern of government repression against environmental activists who challenge large-scale development projects, resource extraction, and government development policies. The report covered a wide spectrum of environmental and development concerns while focusing on civil and political rights violations. The campaign was designed to help recruit new members by addressing issues of concern to the larger environmental movement and to the antiglobalization groups; it has attracted significant support from the movement's grassroots base, particularly among youths.

The campaign was built around three strategic goals: protecting key individual defenders, promoting environmental and human rights standards for corporations operating abroad, and providing protection for affected communities to engage in or resist the effects of development policies. The campaign drew on AI's historic focus on the individual face of rights violations while working to extend existing international standards to enact effective global regulations for corporations. Seeking domestic mechanisms to curtail transnational corporate abuses, the campaign also launched a collaborative effort among development, labor, human rights, and environmental groups to pass "International Right to Know" legislation requiring U.S. corporations operating abroad to disclose information about their environmental impacts, labor practices, and security arrangements (see chapter 4).

The Just Earth! campaign demonstrated the trend toward collaboration between NGOs across movements and sectors. It embraced environmental rights advocacy that long predated the collaboration between two mainstream NGOs, and it signaled the movement of corporate accountability to the mainstream of NGO activity. The initiative enjoyed great popularity with the growing number of young activists in AI-USA. But the campaign did not explicitly address ESC rights. It would take another few years before the next level of strategic change would occur.

2001: Adopting a New Mission. In 1991, AI made the first significant changes in its historic mandate since its founding in 1961. As AI expanded its membership and presence in countries around the world, it became clear that an organization of its size might no longer need operationally to be so limited in its scope, and its historic focus might become indefensible in the face of demands from partnered organizations and AI membership to take on new concerns. Controversy over whether to include sexual orientation as a basis for defining a prisoner of conscience and over other pressing issues led to a mandate review, which opened the door for wider consideration of what human rights AI would work on. The mandate review ultimately led to the adoption of a new mission that would allow work on ESC rights. At the 2001 international decision-making meeting held in Dakar, Senegal, the membership debated and endorsed a limited move toward ESC rights (Matas n.d.).

At a preliminary planning meeting before the 2001 meeting, renowned human rights expert Philip Alston argued that "AI is a civil and political rights organization, not a human rights organization," and that economic and social rights are marginalized. He said that AI has been part of the problem in terms of these rights, and "the [2001] meeting expressed the will that the movement escape from that political and civil rights straitjacket. From Dakar the intention was that indivisibility and interdependence of human rights would have real meaning, that AI would contribute not just to promoting . . . ESC rights, but as well with a limited framework, to prevention and ending their violations" (Matas n.d.).

The changes were immediately visible, and the limited focus identified at the 2001 meeting seems to no longer drive research and advocacy. The organization appears to be fully embracing an ESC rights approach. The introduction of the AI 2005 Annual Report cites the persistence of poverty as "perhaps the gravest threat to human rights and collective security," connecting the new focus on ESC rights to the world's focus on terrorism. Citing the interdependence built into the Universal Declaration of Human Rights and the necessity of recognizing the rights to food, water, and access to an adequate standard of living as equal to civil and political rights, the report states, "The fact that so many people live in inhuman conditions, and that the gap between rich and poor is widening between and within countries, directly contradicts the notion that all human beings are born equal in dignity and rights" (Amnesty International 2005a, 8). Summarizing its country reports, Amnesty cites examples of successful remedies of ESC rights, the linkage between the UN Millennium Development Goals and human rights, and corporate accountability for ESC rights (Amnesty International 2005a).

In 2006, AI began preparing for its first international campaign on ESC rights, to be launched by 2008. The staff at the international secretariat in London defined the options around a wide campaign to popularize the view that ESC rights are human rights or a focus on a particular theme or category of ESC rights, such as the right to health or to water. By mid-2007, the staff had determined that the campaign would focus on human dignity, demonstrating how ESC rights violations lead to poverty.

Focusing on the denial of human rights for those living in poverty and the contribution those violations make to the conditions of poverty, the campaign reinforces the messages coming from the development sector. Poverty is not inevitable. It is a product of decisions by individuals and implemented through policies of states and nonstate actors. A human rights approach identifies the specific violations that lead to conditions of poverty and establishes accountability based on international standards.

The decision to focus largely on poverty for the first international ESC rights campaign was widely debated within Amnesty International sections globally. Fears that it will be difficult to have attainable goals, that AI could be more effective by focusing on a narrower subset of the larger poverty issues, and that donors/constituents will not understand or accept such radical change in focus at this early juncture have all been expressed. Others have argued that the moment is now to stand in solidarity with those fighting the intensification of poverty, and they call for the human rights violations associated with poverty to be recognized by bringing AI's human rights campaigning to strengthen those efforts. Amnesty International, they argue, can contribute at a historic juncture to influencing and supporting rights-based approaches to poverty emanating from the development sector.

How did the organization begin to implement the new mission, including ESC rights? In the past, when AI adopted new areas of work, it built capacity and expertise through pilot projects, drawing on expertise in one region or in one thematic area and expanding it to the wider organization. After the Dakar meeting, AI identified five pilot projects that would cover both diverse geographic regions and different areas of ESC rights. Several of the projects engaged the right to health, an area AI had already begun to move into through a focus on discrimination and protection of health workers. AI's first report reflecting its new work on ESC rights was on health rights for the mentally ill in Bulgaria.

The pilot projects were quickly eclipsed by initiatives that infused ESC rights into country and thematic reports and campaigns. Amnesty International researchers and sections began to focus on the ESC dimensions of existing projects and campaigns, and the positive response helped fuel early support for the ESC rights agenda. The new approach has begun to change Amnesty International's methodologies and identity. The changes necessitated a more strategic approach to planning and required new training and expertise in the staff. Incorporating ESC rights also reinforced the changing identity of AI in relation to the global human rights movement. Historically an NGO that acted on its own, AI increasingly worked in solidarity with other NGOs.

In 2006 an acrimonious debate on sexual and reproductive health, framed in right to health terms, threatened to reverse that trend. The organization is at a crossroads for changing its methodologies and demonstrating its relevance in a dramatically different world order from the one in which it was born. Internally, proponents of a more active role have pushed for the full spectrum approach to the organization's work and have used the defenders model as a way to build common cause with labor, environmental, and development groups.

But the defenders approach, corporate work, and the ESC decision are all part of a decade-long strategic adaptation.

In the preface to the 2001 annual report, secretary-general Pierre Sane summarized the challenges AI had faced in the decade before its fortieth anniversary.

> In a world where globalization is undermining many nation-states and bringing poverty to the forefront of the human rights agenda, the challenge for AI is to remain relevant . . . broadening our aim from the protection of civil and political rights to embrace all human rights. The indivisibility of human rights is not an abstraction: the context which gives rise to human rights violations is invariably complex and cannot be divorced from issues of wealth and status, injustice and impunity.

The significance of this mission change cannot be overstated. Smaller NGOs have worked on ESC rights long before this decision, but AI's endorsement profoundly increases the visibility and legitimacy of ESC approaches to economic globalization. Coupled with new rights-based approaches to development, a common front for applying human rights standards to economic and social policy and poverty issues is emerging.

New NGOs and the Global Network for ESC Rights

As the major international NGOs have moved slowly to develop substantial ESC rights agendas, new organizations and networks have been formed explicitly with an ESC framework. Dynamic and sometimes innovative approaches by networks of NGOs show the potential of ESC rights in fields such as corporate behavior in extractive industries and the rights to water, food, and agrarian reform. Increasingly, ESC rights organizations are applying international human rights standards to national budgets, creating new methods of analyzing and monitoring government policy and actions.[4]

ESC-specific organizations have emerged as national advocacy organizations in Nigeria (SERAC, the Social and Economic Rights

Action Center), Senegal (Association pour le Developpement Economique), Ecuador (Centro de Derechos Economicos y Sociales), New Zealand (The New Zealand Council of Economic, Social and Cultural Rights), Canada (Social Rights Advocacy Center), Korea (Korean Research and Consulting Institute on Poverty), Kenya (Kenya Land Alliance), Brazil (Instituto Brasileiro de Análises Sociais e Econômicas), Portugal (International Centre on Economic, Social and Cultural Rights), and many others.

In the past decade, there has been a proliferation of new organizations formed to promote women's and indigenous peoples' rights and development. These organizations are not exclusively ESC-based groups, and many include civil and political rights seamlessly with their focus on poverty alleviation and sustainable development. In addition, many of the organizations established to promote civil and political rights in countries in the global South also began to incorporate ESC rights into their work, often far earlier than the international human rights NGOs.

In the United States, the Kensington Welfare Rights Union (host to the Poor People's Economic Rights Campaign), National Economic and Social Rights Initiative, the National Center for Human Rights Education, the Women's Institute of Leadership and Development (WILD), and the Mississippi Workers Center for Human Rights are just a few of the organizations that have emerged in the past decade focused on the human rights of marginalized groups in the United States. A new U.S. Network for Human Rights has been founded to link grassroots social justice movements and organizations to the international human rights framework.

Here we will focus on the emergence of international ESC human rights organizations, using case studies of two NGOs and the new international network to link local, national, and international organizations promoting ESC rights. But the real explosion of activity is occurring at the national and community levels in countries throughout the world. These new ESC rights–oriented organizations in the poor countries, together with those operating internationally, are redefining the human rights field.

Among the major centers for developing and testing new strategies are the Food Information and Action Network (FIAN), the Center for Economic and Social Rights (CESR), and the International
Human Rights Council (IHRC). Other international NGOs that are
building their missions to self-consciously address ESC rights as part
of a larger human rights framework, such as Dignity International
or EarthRights International, will be detailed in chapter 4.

THE CENTER FOR ECONOMIC AND SOCIAL RIGHTS

A project on the human rights impact of economic sanctions against
Iraq, launched in 1993 by three law and public health students,
evolved into what is now the Center on Economic and Social Rights
(CESR). CESR's methodology adapts traditional reporting and assessment techniques using a multidisciplinary research approach to fit
the field of ESC rights. It draws together the expertise of the development field in building indices of social and economic inequalities to link to standards of rights. It strives to work with local affected
communities to monitor abuses and to disseminate reports on those
conditions to influence international and national policies. CESR
uses its reporting to gain access to key international bodies such as
UN Commissions, treaty bodies, offices of special rapporteurs, the
Inter-American Court of Human Rights, the European Union, African
Union, and others (Manteris 2003), and it has assisted domestic
NGOs in litigating cases in national courts.

In some projects, CESR has assisted local communities to organize monitoring networks to report on environmental and human
rights abuses associated with oil drilling and mining operations.
CESR cites the significance of engaging affected communities both
from ideological and operational perspectives, and its research
methodology involves direct engagement with local populations and
collaborative relationships with NGOs in the global South.

By the late 1990s, CESR's priority projects included work on extractive industries, the right to water, and education. One project focused
on the impact of mining and oil drilling in several Latin American
countries, highlighting the growing awareness of violations of ESC

rights by the development projects of the 1970s and 1980s. Led by Centro de Derechos Economicos y Sociales (CDES) in Quito, Ecuador, coordinating with regional indigenous groups, the project amplified the concerns of local communities and movements that development projects were creating conditions for violations and should be accountable to international standards of human rights.

CESR played an important leadership role in promoting the recognition of the right to water as a human right and calling attention to the impact of industrialization, privatization, and pollution on diminished access to clean, affordable, and healthy water for the majority of the world's population. CESR also has projects in the United States, using the right to education to challenge the city of New York under international human rights standards to guarantee that education provided to city children meets certain minimum standards. CESR was also a participant in and supported the development of the Poor People's Economic Human Rights Campaign in the United States.

In 2005, with the departure of its founders, CESR developed a new strategic plan for organizational focus and expansion. It recently announced that it would expand its offices from sole headquarters based in New York to open new offices in Spain along with other offices in fields of operation to project a global identity. It is also moving more aggressively into the area of measurement of international economic and social rights standards, citing the need for rigorous methods of assessment in campaigning and litigation. In another critical role, CESR has served as the home base of the ESCR-Net project, detailed below.

THE CENTRE ON HOUSING RIGHTS AND EVICTIONS

The Centre on Housing Rights and Evictions (COHRE) was founded in 1994 to promote and protect the full enjoyment of economic, social, and cultural rights, with a particular focus on the human right to adequate housing and preventing forced evictions. Now operating offices in Switzerland, Ghana, Brazil, Thailand, Australia, the Netherlands, Sri Lanka, South Africa, and the United States, COHRE has explicitly evolved as an international NGO, representing and collaborating with grassroots movements, community-based organizations, and domestic NGOs around the world. Managing geographically based programs (Americas, Africa, Asia) and thematic programs (housing property and restitution, women and housing rights, right to water, forced evictions monitoring and advocacy, and the ESC rights litigation), COHRE receives the majority of its funding from European foundations and governments, but it also receives funding from foundations in the United States and in countries where it works.

The geographic programs work with NGOs and community-based organizations to conduct fact-finding missions, train local groups in rights standards, and provide technical support for national and international advocacy. COHRE collaborates with community groups and national NGOS to educate them on the process of bringing housing rights to the attention of appropriate UN agencies and treaty bodies. The COHRE Africa Program, for example, has partnered with the Social and Economic Rights Action Center (SERAC) in Lagos, Nigeria.

COHRE has been at the forefront of developing litigation strategies and promoting the argument that clear remedies to ESC rights violations exist. For instance, working with the Australian Human Rights Center, COHRE published a series of studies on the emerging body of case law on ESC rights and on the impact of litigation in national, regional, and international courts. It also offers case studies on how international institutions have been sued, establishing international accountability for ESC rights violations in national contexts (Squires, Langford, and Thiele 2005). COHRE also produces the *Housing and ESC Rights Law Quarterly* and a frequently updated publication containing leading ESC rights cases from around the world.

COHRE's ESC rights litigation program supports and promotes litigation by publishing resources, maintaining case law databases, intervening before courts, tribunals and international bodies, giving legal advice to NGOs and others, providing training, maintaining a global network of lawyers, and advocating for better complaint mechanisms.[5] In turn, it has developed training programs for public interest lawyers in developing countries and for justices and members of parliament involved in legislation or adjudication of housing rights claims.

COHRE's Right to Water Programme emerged out of advocacy for the recognition of a "new" right by the UN Committee on ESC rights, adopted through General Comment No. 15 and now internationally recognized as a human right. Subsequent litigation strategies have focused on implementing this right through regional human rights mechanisms and by national governments.[6] In 2003, COHRE collaborated with the World Health Organization, the UN high commissioner for human rights, WaterAid, and CESR to publish *The Right to Water*, an excellent review of the emergence of the "new" right to water and the meaning of the UN General Comment (World Health Organization 2004). The right to water is discussed further in chapter 4.

While using traditional fact-finding and litigation methods, COHRE has built a grassroots network of more than fifteen hundred organizations and conducts grassroots education initiatives and campaigns. Like CESR, COHRE explicitly builds local partnerships around the right to adequate housing, relying on the expertise of local organizations to conduct its research and programs.

COHRE has developed its newer, more expansive focus, building upon its historic housing mission, out of recognition of the interdependence of rights. While explicitly focused on ESC rights, COHRE's reports, litigation, and human rights education reinforce the interdependence of the right to housing with the right to be free from arbitrary or unlawful interference in the home (Article 17 of the International Covenant on Civil and Political Rights, Article 8 of the European Convention for the Protection of Human Rights and Fundamental Freedoms, and Article 11 of the American Convention on Human Rights) and with the right to property (delineated in Article 21 of the American Convention on Human Rights, Article 1 of the First Protocol to the European Convention for the Protection of Human Rights and Fundamental Freedoms, and Article 14 of the African Charter on Human and Peoples' Rights).[7]

ESCR-Net

In June 2003 the inaugural conference of the ESCR-Net was held in Chiang Mai, Thailand. The conference brought together 250 activists from fifty countries, and it culminated two years of preparation and global consultations by launching a global network dedicated to promoting the principle that all human rights are universal, indivisible and interdependent, and to rectifying the historic inattention to economic, social, and cultural rights. ESCR-Net's explicit commitment to promoting the participation of social movements, not simply NGOs, demonstrates the significance that grassroots social movements have had in promoting ESC rights, in contrast to international or national NGOs.

The network's decentralized structure allows participants around the world to share strategies, resources, and experiences to build more coherent and powerful tools for ESC rights advocacy, without the dominance of large international NGOs. Currently, two working groups focus on corporate accountability and on social movements and grassroots groups. Thematic discussion groups focus on women's economic, social, and cultural rights; trade and investment and human rights; and the right to health.

Projects undertaken by the network include budget analysis and human rights, export credit agencies and human rights, optional protocol for the International Covenant on Economic, Social and Cultural Rights that would allow for individual complaint mechanisms, and the development of a case law database. The budget analysis project has grown rapidly, as national NGOs and movements use analytic tools and human rights standards to monitor and challenge government allocation of resources for social and economic policies (www.ESCR-Net.org). The consultation process that preceded the launch of the network was supported by funds from the Ford Foundation.[8]

Debating ESC Rights Advocacy

As partners in the global South continue to pressure the international human rights NGOs to expand their work on ESC rights, and as specialized ESC rights NGOs and grassroots campaigns on economic and social policies within a human rights framework continue to proliferate, the debate on how, how far, and how effective international NGOs can be in promoting economic and social rights continues to rage (Yamin 2005).

The debate revolves around four central questions. First, can the historic methods of human rights advocacy, developed to advance civil and political rights, be effective in economic and social rights advocacy? Second, can effective standards be established for measuring government attainment of ESC rights? Third, do international NGOs have the same legitimacy in pursuing ESC rights or is their promotion best left to domestic constituencies? Finally, can international human rights NGOs effectively expand their activities to include a wider range of issues, or will they dilute their effectiveness, stretch their resources, and confuse their constituencies?

Many of these debates among practitioners occur in the context of organizational deliberations about changing mandates and across the professional and volunteer ranks of human rights activists, but some of these debates appear in the public record or in published exchanges among human rights practitioners. One such exchange occurred in the pages of *Human Rights Quarterly*, a journal that engages academics and practitioners alike (Roth 2004; Rubenstein 2004; Robinson 2004). The articles cited represented key arguments and perspectives from within the traditional U.S.-based human rights organizations and United Nations agencies that have historically worked on civil and political rights.

DO TRADITIONAL METHODS APPLY?

Kenneth Roth, executive director of Human Rights Watch, published a widely read article outlining concerns about the relevance of the methods traditionally employed by international human rights NGOs when applied to economic and social rights advocacy. While Roth and Human Rights Watch embrace moving into ESC rights work, he argues for a limited application of what he perceives as the human rights methodology to economic and social rights (Roth 2004). His arguments about the relevance of methodology also question whether ESC rights standards can be established with the same clarity as civil and political rights, as well as whether clear remedies can be established for ESC rights violations.

Roth first identifies the human rights methodology as primarily "naming and shaming" targets, documenting human rights abuses, and mobilizing international pressure to enforce those rights through mechanisms much like the "boomerang" model identified by Keck and Sikkink (1998).

He argues that most of the ESC rights advocacy to date has been rhetorical, largely lacking concrete analysis of who are the duty holders for these rights, failing to identify the specific acts or policies that constitute violations of ESC rights, and displaying only limited analysis of what constitutes "progressive realization" of ESC rights, the standard obligation of all state parties to the ICESCR.[9] Roth argues that human rights NGOs provide little added value when their advocacy is not grounded in investigation and research, and that making moral claims with little substance risks dissipating their own finite political capital.

Roth argues for an approach to ESC rights that builds on the methodological strength of international human rights groups—the ability to investigate, expose, and shame. That is done most effectively when governmental or corporate conduct can be held to scrutiny and where there is a clear, identifiable violation, violator, and remedy. As he argues, "If any of these three elements is missing, our capacity to shame is greatly diminished . . . who is responsible for the violations and what is the remedy? These answers flow much less directly from the mere documentations of ESC rights violations, than they do in the civil and political rights realm." Using the example of a substandard public health system, he argues that the target government and the international community likely contribute to the violation, and that the complexity of the issue reduces the power of traditional human rights methods.

Roth further argues that given such complexity, human rights organizations focusing on ESC rights should direct their work to cases of arbitrary or discriminatory government conduct that directly contributes to ESC rights violations. International human rights groups should not engage in ESC rights advocacy in areas of "distributive justice," where the main focus is how budgetary dollars are allocated. If the target has a credible rebuttal, citing debt burden or terms of trade as constraining factors, then the credibility of the NGOs will be damaged and the work will be perceived as futile. But when research can demonstrate that discriminatory or exclusionary policies resulted in rights violations, then activists are in a position to employ the naming and shaming methodology that has been so successful in winning international support.

Roth articulates a historic challenge posed by critics of ESC rights advocacy. When coupled with the fact that human rights NGOs have finite resources and face spiraling civil and political rights emergencies worldwide, this argument wins substantial support. But in a politically charged debate, Roth's carefully crafted argument was immediately denounced as simplistic and regressive by many ESC rights proponents, and it was interpreted as arguing that if ESC rights cannot fit within the existing methodologies, then they are not legitimate human rights. Roth's arguments were also seen as challenging the legitimacy of the claims by those who are suffering from economic and social rights violations, and the article unleashed an emotional debate within the human rights NGO community.

Emotions aside, the substance of Roth's argument on methodology was dissected by many at the forefront of the ESC rights movement. Roth's methodological argument in effect defines the human rights agenda as those issues on which an existing human rights methodology can be employed effectively. If traditional human rights methodology does not fit neatly with new human rights challenges, the argument goes, then the new conditions do not warrant the work. In fact, the central response to Roth's argument has been that the methodology may apply in some circumstances, but may need to be altered in other, changed conditions, whether for work on civil and political rights or on ESC rights.

Mary Robinson (2004), former UN high commissioner for human rights, published a response calling for a more nuanced understanding of the human rights methodology. "In the interest that ESC rights are taken more seriously as obligations," she argues, "international human rights organizations should not be unduly limited in identifying the targets of their naming and the means of their shaming." She goes on to argue that governments, corporations, and international financial institutions can be named and shamed and can be subjects of other methods of mobilization that advance the realization of ESC rights (Robinson 2004, 870). Robinson denies that there is an inevitable tradeoff among ESC rights in government spending priorities. Rather, she argues, human rights advocates can lobby for greater allocation of resources for progressive realization of rights when government resources exist but are siphoned away by corruption, misspending, or unnecessary military expenditures.

Robinson's argument is reinforced by Yamin's (2005) call for reconceptualization of human rights methods to advance ESC rights in ways that account for changed international conditions and changed power relations between the state and economic actors. It is possible to identify multiple violators while determining both accountability and remedy for the abuses. Yamin (2005, 1231) cites a report by Public Citizen on water privatization in Ghana that examined the shared responsibility of the IMF, the World Bank, the Ghanaian government, and the British Department for International Development for violations of rights to health, life, and water. NGOs largely based in the global South have focused on subjecting international institutions and trade and commercial regimes to human rights assessments, requiring a blending of traditional civil and political methods with development tools.

In another response, Leonard Rubenstein of Physicians for Human Rights addresses the concern that the violation, the violator, and the remedy are unclear in ESC rights. Rubenstein argues that international human rights groups can monitor state compliance with increasingly explicit obligations to ESC rights and generate the level of international outrage required for effectiveness. Such international outrage can be aroused with respect to government discrimination in delivery of services, as well to the policies of international institutions that shape economic conditions in target countries.

Roth's arguments against campaigning on distributive justice issues rest in essence on the difficulty of establishing standards for ESC rights attainment. The argument goes back to the early days of deliberation on implementing treaties for the Universal Declaration of Human Rights, but Rubenstein argues that there is now clarity on how to measure government obligations to respect, protect, and fulfill rights, and the obligations need not devolve to questions of distributive justice, but can focus on the level of investment by governments and the design of policies and programs.

Developing effective recommendations, Rubenstein argues, requires an expanded understanding of "the human rights methodology" that goes beyond naming and shaming. International NGOs are already collaborating with organizations in the global South to lobby for policies, systems, and services that can fulfill ESC rights, and human rights organizations, which have historically worked to develop institutions that can protect and fulfill rights, can apply their experience in this area to ESC rights.

Institution building in the civil and political field has had a domestic component and an international component, as shown by the advocacy for an international justice system to hold perpetrators of past violations accountable. ESC rights advocacy will require similar understanding of how stronger institutions, national and international, can bring about greater compliance with ESC obligations. "In many cases, instead of seeking to embarrass governments, institution-building strategies seek to win them over." (Rubenstein 2004, 851). Such an approach requires a complex strategy that understands when governments are targets and when they are partners in the achievement of rights, whether civil and political or ESC, a topic we will return to in the conclusion.

International human rights organizations are advocating for expanded governmental resources essential to meet ESC rights. Again this is not a new area. Rubenstein further argues that remedies for civil and political rights violations have often included recommendations for expanded government investment in judicial capacity, better training for police, more prisons, etc. Ironically, recommendations for civil and political redress that involved government expenditures were often made with no attention to budgetary considerations. Human rights groups, he shows, are also working with international donors to design development programs with an understanding of their human rights implications. International human rights NGOs can support governments in designing economic and social policies that meet both core obligations and progressive realization standards. Naming and shaming techniques will be employed in some cases, institution and capacity building in others, and at some times both simultaneously.

By employing a human rights approach, economic recommendations should not result in a tradeoff between categories of ESC rights. A human rights approach focused on governments' obligations to respect, protect, and fulfill ESC rights will necessarily incorporate analysis of discriminatory practices in implementation of economic and social policies, while ensuring that policies will not inadvertently harm others. Rubenstein cites the example of work on HIV/AIDS that has required governments to ensure that health professionals have not been diverted away from other populations or other acute health needs.

International human rights NGOs are understandably at an early stage in detailing the affirmative obligation of states to meet basic needs, and, as Rubenstein argues, they will require new strategies and methods to pressure governments, including more sophisticated capacities for understanding the design and impact of social programs and the design of budgets and social service systems (Rubenstein 2004, 855). Human rights analysis of budgets has become an important new tool for ESC rights advocacy. ESCR-Net formed a working group on budget analysis and ESC rights, explicitly addressing the interest of its member organizations in analysis of how states can fulfill ESC rights through allocation of public resources. ESCR-Net also developed an initiative in partnership with Dignity International, the International Budget Project, and International Human Rights Internship Project to form the Linking and Learning Project on Budget Analysis and ESCR. The project offers an annual training in budget analysis for human rights practitioners, and in 2004 the three organizations produced a training document titled "Dignity Counts: A Guide to Using Budget Analysis to Advance Human Rights" (www.internationalbudget.org/themes/ESC).

But who is the violator? In response to Roth's other major criticism, Rubenstein argues that NGOs have already demonstrated the applicability of their naming and shaming methodology to multiple targets in reference to ESC rights violations. Rubenstein cites the campaigns on the right to essential medicines, where naming and shaming pressured pharmaceutical companies and governments to remove barriers to greater availability of generic HIV/AIDS drugs (see chapter 4). Others argue that these campaigns are beginning to implement the intent of Article 2 of the ICESCR, establishing international accountability for attainment of ESC rights in third-party countries by targeting rich-country donors and corporate actors. Already many international human rights NGOs have called on rich-donor countries to expand contributions to international funds with rights and development functions, such as the United Nations Fund to Fight Tuberculosis, Malaria and HIV/AIDS.

CAN SHAME BE MOBILIZED?

Perhaps the issue most important to whether the naming and shaming method works for ESC rights was not addressed in published debates on the issue. Can shame be mobilized for ESC rights in Western countries where development is predominantly viewed as market-driven and charity-based, rather than subject to human rights accountability? The rights-based approach transcends economic paradigms because the focus is on standards of attainment, irrespective of the characteristics of the economic system. Effective pressure for international accountability for rights violations in third countries, and pressure on nonstate economic actors to change policies that have ESC rights impacts, will require a constituency for ESC rights. There is not yet enough experience with efforts to mobilize shame at the global level around ESC rights to begin to make a judgment. There is early evidence that such mobilizations can work, as AI reports and urgent action alerts over forced evictions have generated substantial response by its membership. Empirical research will be essential for assessing the power and effectiveness of the new rights approaches of traditional human rights NGOs.

The public constituency for ESC rights in the wealthy industrial countries varies greatly. Northern European countries have a history of public commitment to social development and the welfare state in their own societies, coupled with tremendous financial support for development policies based on their interpretation of international responsibilities. This is not the case in the United States.

DO INTERNATIONAL NGOs HAVE LEGITIMACY TO WORK ON ESC RIGHTS?

Due to the detailed analysis of social policy and budgetary allocations inherent in ESC rights advocacy, Roth and others argue that international human rights organizations do not have the same moral authority in making recommendations on ESC rights issues as on civil and political rights. International human rights NGOs, for instance, can demand that governments stop torturing, but can they legitimately recommend that a government spend more on health care and, perhaps, less on education?

Rubenstein and Robinson both argue that work on ESC rights requires a different type of partnership with community-based and national organizations. International human rights NGOs have been criticized for decades for not working closely and collaboratively with domestic social justice and human rights organizations, whether focused on civil and political rights, economic and social rights, or on establishing priorities. The explosion of activity in the global South on human rights, which predated the international NGO debates over ESC rights, has already fundamentally challenged the notion of collaboration and called upon international NGOs to restructure their methodologies in response.

Perhaps the real argument that should take place is whether international human rights NGOs have the legitimacy to work on civil and political rights if they don't work on ESC rights. Human rights activists in the global South have put considerable pressure on international human rights NGOs to adopt agendas and strategies that take the interdependence of rights seriously. This pressure, together with changes in the international system, has produced a fairly rapid strategic adjustment by leading international NGOs.

CAN HUMAN RIGHTS INTERNATIONAL NGOs BE EFFECTIVE WITH AN EXPANDED MANDATE?

Given the magnitude of human rights violations worldwide, can organizations have a "full spectrum" approach to human rights with finite resources and limited constituencies? Six years after Amnesty International voted to embrace an expanded range of human rights work to include advocacy on ESC rights, Amnesty International activists' fundamental critique of that move is that the movement may not be able to cover all human rights violations. Faced with the human rights violations in the war on terror, with backsliding by Western governments on civil and political rights guarantees such as the use of torture and the rights of due process, expanding mandates to include economic and social rights is now even more daunting and controversial. The challenge of addressing expanded priorities is a familiar one for human rights organizations and is often articulated in AI as a choice between the expanded mission and the forgotten prisoner: how can AI take on new issues while there are still prisoners of conscience that have not been freed? Reflecting that same concern, Human Rights First made a calculated decision to retreat from its growing advocacy on ESC rights to accommodate an increase in campaigning on human rights abuses associated with the war on terror. It remains unclear whether this will become a permanent position.

But the debate is not merely one of priorities. It contains within it deep differences on the validity of ESC rights advocacy. Nonetheless, concern about the investment in new capacity needed to document ESC rights is real, as is the worry that grassroots lobbying capacity will be spread thin over an expanded agenda. There is reason for concern, as expressed among Amnesty International members, for example, that ESC rights activism will make it more difficult

to distinguish AI from the growing number of NGOs working on development, environment, and global peace. This prospect intensifies
concerns that ESC advocacy may diminish the capacity of international human rights NGOs to protect freedoms worldwide.

Would it be preferable to have a range of specialized human rights
organizations focused on subsets of rights issues, to build constituencies, expertise, and credibility to lobby and mobilize on behalf of
those rights? Is there a place for NGOs that work broadly on a "full
spectrum" of human rights issues while risking possible diffusion
and superficial expertise? Does specialization negate the indivisibility of rights and risk establishing priorities among rights that do not
square with the daily lives of the majority of the world's population?

The debate on relevance and efficacy will continue as organizations
work through their own approaches to an expanded or focused human rights mission. Ultimately, and perhaps paradoxically, the issue
of relevance to the lives of the majority of the world's population has
driven support for ESC rights advocacy and fueled this new movement. NGOs will continue to respond to pressure to embrace ESC
rights as a tool for addressing economic and social change worldwide.

Impact of the New Movement for ESC Rights

For the human rights field, the significance of these trends is twofold.
First, collaboration with development and environmental NGOs offers a way to address economic globalization issues through human
rights campaigning, in collaboration with NGOs that have been leading current mobilizations. Second, and more significantly, the global
movement for ESC rights and the growing adoption of a "full spectrum" approach validates and gives concrete operational meaning to
the concepts of "interdependence" and "indivisibility" of rights. To
date, indivisibility has been an abstraction for NGOs, who prioritize
sets of rights in their activities while rhetorically upholding the concept of a unified whole.

NGOs' embrace of strategies to secure political participation, to uti-
lize accepted international standards to alleviate growing poverty,

and to render corporations accountable to the development, environmental, and human rights impact of their operations is a clearer and more explicit effort to exercise power than many international NGO initiatives in the past. International human rights NGOs' assertion of the relevance and authority of human rights standards, and their growing collaboration with other sectors (analyzed in chapter 4), are expressions of a clear desire to multiply their influence over governments and economic actors.

Finally, "human rights" provides a proactive and positive vision of important social movement and NGO agendas. If NGOs are to contribute effectively to reversing the harshest effects of economic globalization, they must shift the characterization of their activities as "antiglobalization." By upholding a universal and indivisible framework for human dignity and freedom, and making explicit its implications for particular policy issues and areas of corporate conduct, human rights NGOs may be able to inspire popular support, integrate advocacy movements, and succeed in holding economic actors to standards previously applied only to governments.

Taken together, two forces are changing the human rights field profoundly. Unlike the development sector, where change could be ephemeral, the move to embrace ESC rights cannot be characterized as a fad for international human rights NGOs. Grassroots advocacy for ESC rights globally is altering the way human rights supporters think about human rights today. It will not easily be reversed. Such change has already begun to alter the discourse of rights among practitioners and increasingly, even academics in the West. If international NGOs that both have sustained partnerships in the global South and that have embraced some level of advocacy on ESC rights were to reverse their direction, they are vulnerable to the charge that they are creating a new bifurcation of rights and undercutting the very principles of indivisibility and interdependence that is at the normative core of the international system of rights. For those organizations that acknowledged their neglect of ESC rights, a visible move away from ESC rights advocacy would delegitimize them in the eyes of their global counterparts and in the eyes of some

Western supporters. Thus, the sector-wide durability of this move seems likely, even if some organizations have a weak adoption of ESC rights or retreat from it to respond to other crises. However, effectiveness and impact are very much still in question.

Long-term evaluation will indicate whether commonality with development NGOs blurs human rights missions, erodes support, and confuses constituencies. Rigorous monitoring of these trends will assess whether NGOs can succeed in building support for the new methodologies and translate that support into concrete and effective programs and successful advocacy.

Notes

1. Bret Thiele, coordinator of ESC Rights Litigation Programme at Centre on Housing Rights and Evictions (COHRE), interview with Ellen Dorsey.
2. Michael Posner, telephone interview by Catherine Griebel, September 2, 2003.
3. Michael Posner, telephone interview by Catherine Griebel, September 2, 2003.
4. See the Global Learning Programme on Budget Analysis and ESC Rights, Dignity International and ESC Rights Network.
5. Bret Thiele, director of COHRE ESC Rights Litigation Programme, interview.
6. Bret Thiele, interview, March 16, 2003, and August 23, 2006.
7. Bret Thiele, interview, March 16, 2003, and August 23, 2006.
8. Ford's former senior program officer for human rights, Larry Cox, has been instrumental in developing, supporting, and connecting ESC rights organizations, activists, and movements, and in introducing other funders to the growing ESC rights movement. Cox is now executive director of Amnesty International USA.
9. All state parties to ICESCR are obligated to meet minimum standards of ESC rights attainment, while demonstrating progressive realization (or improvement) of those rights over time.

3

NGOs AND
THE DEVELOPMENT INDUSTRY
Toward a Rights-Based Approach?

*W*hat is a rights-based approach? It is a
lens and an approach to all our work, be
that programming or within our own
organisation. A rights-based approach deliberately and
explicitly focuses on people achieving the minimum
conditions for living with dignity (i.e. achieving their
human rights). It does so by exposing the roots of
vulnerability and marginalization and expanding the
range of responses. It empowers people to claim and
exercise their rights and fulfill their responsibilities. A
rights-based approach recognises poor, displaced, and
war-affected people as having inherent rights essential
to livelihood security—rights that are (sometimes)
validated by law.

—CARE International UK, 2005

Introduction
The development field is at a pivotal juncture. As development assistance became increasingly directed by post–cold war democracy
promotion, market-based free trade and investment policies, and
humanitarian crises and antiterrorist battles on several fronts, aid
practitioners have sought out initiatives and strategies to reawaken
the priority of poverty eradication. Human rights–based development has become an attractive option and is receiving a great deal
of attention, particularly from practitioners (Alston and Robinson
2005, Alsop 2005, Gready and Ensor 2005, Oxfam America and

89

CARE USA 2007). It proposes to shift the practice of development by subjecting it to evaluation by internationally recognized standards and principles and by placing governments' development policies, as well as donors' development assistance, within a framework of rights, entitlements, obligations, and accountability.

This chapter addresses three issues raised by this turn of events in development and by the groundswell of interest in human rights–based approaches. First, we explore the origins of interest in human rights–based approaches, arguing that both substantive concerns about poverty, the desire for an alternative to unregulated market solutions to economic and social problems, and organizational preoccupations with image and positioning are essential to understanding the trend.

There has been a small undercurrent of human rights–based approaches throughout the history of development, but the discussion has been largely confined to United Nations and regional bodies, legal scholars, and a handful of specialized NGOs and institutes. The present interest in rights-based development is broader in scope, more concrete in its application by social movements and citizen organizations, and more specific. Advocates not only promote the broad rights to food, housing, health, and education, but also more specific policy issues within those sectors, including agrarian reform, access to essential medicines, and the privatization of water systems.

Second, we analyze the issues troubling development as a field— failures of impact and accountability, the dominance of neoliberal doctrine, and the growing corporate profile in development assistance—and argue that human rights approaches offer distinctive solutions to each element of development's woes. Human rights–based approaches have the potential, their advocates claim, to transform development from an expression of generosity and of power by wealthy donors to a set of clear expectations and obligations for all governments and all actors in development to respect internationally recognized rights.

The gaps between theory and contemporary practice are the third theme of this chapter, as we trace the variety of forms of implementation aid agencies and NGOs have followed. The current mélange of strategies risks squandering the potential and confirming the suspicions of many in the aid industry that human rights standards are of limited use for setting social policy and for making real decisions about the use and allocation of resources. The chapter concludes with a reflection on the durability, potential, constraints, and limits of human rights–based approaches in the development field and on the conditions that would be required to fulfill their potential.

Organizations, Politics, and the Meaning of Rights-Based Approaches

Since the mid-1990s, human rights–based approaches have been among the most discussed movements in development. Donors such as the UNDP and UNICEF, Swedish Sida and British DFID, and NGOs and networks of NGOs such as Save the Children, CARE, ActionAid, and Oxfam have declared themselves as rights-based agencies. Think tanks including the London-based Overseas Development Institute, Norway's Christian Michelsen Institute, the Swedish Ministry of Foreign Affairs, Institute for Development Studies at the University of Sussex, and NGO umbrella organizations such as InterAction in the United States and BOND in the United Kingdom, have convened meetings or published briefings.

Human rights strategies have an obvious appeal for activist NGOs critical of orthodox development: international standards provide a basis for their ongoing critique of neoliberal development practice. But development NGOs that have historically cooperated with mainstream governmental donor agencies have also embraced rights-based approaches. CARE International and Save the Children have both adopted new human rights–driven strategies, and World Vision has cautiously and strategically embraced a human rights framework in analyzing and addressing children's issues.

To understand the embrace of human rights approaches, one must understand international development NGOs both as political actors and as organizations with their own internal needs and imperatives. International NGOs' adoption of rights-based approaches is a strategic response to changes in the organizations' environment. Development NGOs react to political and economic changes that affect their work and its impact, and they also react to pressures from funders and perceived competitors and to trends in the field as manifested in the work of leading agencies and influential thinkers and writers.

As political actors, NGOs are seeking to counter neoliberal development models and to embrace the standards and assertion of human dignity associated with human rights. As organizations, they also need to protect the development enterprise, under fire from both the political left and right, and maintain their own credibility (Dimaggio and Powell 1983) and protect access to resources (Pfeffer and Salancik 1978). Organizations weigh and balance competing demands and bids for influence and control, and much of any organization's behavior is driven by coping with these demands and with the expectations and fashions of a society or a profession.

Given the diversity of development organizations, and of their imperatives, it is no surprise that there is no single, coherent rights-based approach, but a range of tentative and highly varied commitments among development agencies. The UN agencies such as UNDP and UNICEF, and NGOs such as CARE, ActionAid, Oxfam, and Save the Children, have proceeded in highly varied and uneven manners, as have the national, bilateral agencies such as British DFID and Swedish Sida. Plipat's (2005) study of development NGOs and bilateral agencies demonstrates the wide range of variation among these approaches.

Skeptics argue that the rhetoric and trappings of rights-based development are much more in evidence than is any clarity about what exactly the rights-based approach means for actual programs and projects. Some argue that "rights-based development" is simply a slogan to sum up a set of values, trends, and initiatives in development practice, a metaphor that "catalyses a set of values into a phrase that many people can adapt and adopt" (Pratt 2003, 2). But Joachim Theis (2003) of Save the Children–Sweden offers a two-part definition of the rights-based approach, which we will adopt, that defines the rights-based approach in terms of its objectives, and its standards and methods:

A rights-based approach to development promotes justice,
equality and freedom and tackles the power issues that lie at the
root of poverty and exploitation. To achieve this, a rights-based
approach makes use of the standards, principles and methods of
human rights, social activism, and of development (Theis 2003).

There is, in other words, a politics of the rights-based approach as
well as a methodology. Politically, the rights-based approach involves
commitments to egalitarian strategies, to addressing causes of poverty
and exclusion, and to meaningful participation in decision making.
These commitments are wholly consistent with human rights approaches, but they are not unique to human rights–based approaches, and many development agencies embrace such values and
practices without specifically affirming human rights.

The *methods* of a rights-based approach, however, tie it to international human rights agreements, standards, and principles. Fully
implementing a rights-based approach means embracing the authoritative internationally agreed standards of the major human rights instruments and applying these standards and principles in the agency's
core activities: designing and implementing projects, strengthening
donors' and governments' accountability to them, advocating policies that protect and advance their achievement, educating about human rights standards, and promoting the capacity of rights holders
to demand their rights and duty bearers (states) to meet them. Human rights–based development initiatives are not only grounded
philosophically in internationally recognized human rights, they are
identified, designed, implemented, monitored, and evaluated with
reference to those human rights standards.

Rights-based development work, then, involves at least these four
commitments: to meaningful, influential participation for people
affected by programs; to addressing root causes of poverty and exclusion; to expanding the authority of and respect for human rights standards; and to addressing the issues of discrimination and exclusion. It
pursues these commitments by explicit reference to internationally
recognized human rights standards and principles and to their expression in national constitutions and statutes. Finally, where agencies

work primarily through partnerships and grant making to local organizations, their choices of local "partner" agencies will reflect a commitment to advancing human rights.

Concern for human rights requires attention to the roles of governments in fulfilling them, and therefore a re-emphasis on advocacy. Development support, which has historically meant material assistance through projects, programs, and policy advocacy to shape the practice of development aid, has taken on a broader meaning as the rapid expansion of international trade and reorganization of the productive economy often leaves poor countries with dramatically diminished opportunities. Development support increasingly means participating in the rule-making process that governs trade and finance. This sometimes means putting pressure on aid-receiving governments to conform to human rights standards, mobilizing international pressure, and mirroring the practice of civil and political human rights advocacy. But advocacy on economic and social policy also involves confronting international agencies and transnational corporations with their obligations to respect, protect, and promote the fulfillment of human rights (Brysk 2005; Nelson and Dorsey 2007).

This advocacy role is being thrust upon organizations in a development field that has been reluctant to engage directly with contentious international issues that directly challenge power relations. In the development industry at large, the tendency to avoid politics and power in favor of a discourse of technical expertise, correct institutions, and proper policies has been well documented (Ferguson 1990; Nelson 1995). International development NGOs, too, have generally favored "service delivery rather than advocacy" (Lindenberg and Bryant 2001, 173) and have focused much of their advocacy on calling attention to particular crises or calling for more generous aid spending, rather than on challenging structural and institutional causes of poverty and inequality (Lindenberg and Bryant 2001).

Development as a field is undeniably subject to fashion. But the adoption of rights-based approaches should be watched closely and critically because human rights–based development proposes, *in principle,* a significant, qualitative change in the entire outlook of development. Other changes in development policy have proposed new priorities for governments and donors; integrated rural development, basic human needs, sustainable development and human development, for example, all assert new priorities for development aid and policy. But like neoliberal development doctrine of the 1980s, which called for a fundamental change from state-directed development planning to market-driven development and a sharply reduced regulatory role for the state, human rights–driven development does something more. It calls for a new set of rules for development practice, a reconceptualization that involves a radical change in the authority and power behind the development industry. By calling for governments' policy and donors' projects and programs to be accountable to a set of standards and principles, and by acknowledging the authority of internationally recognized standards, rights-based development would give poor people's organizations and movements a source of leverage in demanding improved services, transparent decision making, meaningful participation and freedom from discriminatory treatment, and real accountability over policy outcomes.

In short, a rights-based approach moves development from its present framework—international goal setting and charity driven by enlightened self-interest—to entitlement to a quality of life for all individuals, based in an internationally recognized set of standards that governments and international institutions have specific obligations to meet.

The Development Field and the Call for Rights-Based Approaches

To understand how human rights–based approaches have been received among development agencies, one needs to recall the history of shifting and evolving fashions in the field. Sixty years of fads and fashions, new theories, technologies, and slogans have disappointed observers, participants, and "beneficiaries," and new initiatives are now greeted with skepticism in many quarters (see e.g., Escobar 1995; Dichter 2001; Isbister 1998). With each new fashion, aid agencies adopt new approaches, incorporate the new buzzwords into programs and documents, and join new interagency working groups. Development has arrived at an impasse whose dimensions—skepticism about impact, accountability, corporate globalization, and the compromised independence of NGOs—make human rights–based approaches particularly attractive.

Sociologist Stephen Browne (2000) traces the history of development assistance through four eras: development as growth, as basic human needs, as liberalization, and as NGOs and good governance. The typology captures the movement of aid donors toward the current environment of frustration and dissent over neoliberal policies and the shoring up of the neoliberal model with a patchwork of strategies involving governance, NGOs, targeted social investments, and market-friendly reforms. (Browne's book appeared at the beginning of what might be a fifth development "era," one decisively shaped by human rights. Whether this turns out to be so remains to be seen.)

The theory and practice of development as economic growth in the 1950s and 1960s was driven by the belief that capital investment could help a growing agrarian economy "take off" into rapid economic growth and industrialization (Rostow 1960). Troubled by slow progress in reducing global poverty and hunger, development practitioners shifted emphasis in the 1970s toward agriculture, health, education, and other services to improve well-being among the poor and stimulate growth in the sectors where they worked. "Basic human needs" and "redistribution with growth" dominated development agencies in the 1970s, but they were swept aside by the neoliberal revolution in the early 1980s.

Neoliberal theorists in the United States, the United Kingdom, and the World Bank believed that aid programs would continue to fail until governments removed the flawed policies that distorted economies and created disincentives to investment and exports. Two decades of aid programs beginning in 1980 featured policy conditions to cut government spending and employment, privatize government-owned enterprises, and create incentives for trade and investment. The World Bank, the most influential proponent of neoliberal strategies, used its financial leverage as well as personal, intellectual, and professional networks of influence to win at least partial implementation of the free-market agenda (Mosley 1995; Goldman 2005).

The profile of NGOs in the aid sector skyrocketed during the same period, as donors enlisted both national and international NGOs' services to replace government-provided social services and help manage emergency social funds and social investment funds designed to soften the human impact of rapid economic reform. Although some international development NGOs were troubled by the role voluntary agencies were playing in the dismantling of government enterprises and agencies, NGOs participated in nearly all of 108 such funds financed by the World Bank in fifty-seven countries between 1987 and 1995 (World Bank 1999), and NGO roles in managing projects funded by other major bilateral donors also grew rapidly (Lewis 2001, 62–64).

The "new" development agenda of the 1990s—sustainable growth, broadly based growth, and good governance—softened the single-minded focus of the 1980s, but it was still market-driven. Good governance, for example, in World Bank terms, promotes popular participation, judicial reform, anticorruption strategies, transparency and accountability, and improvements in public management, and it justifies each of these by its hoped-for positive impact on foreign investment and on the efficiency of transactions in the economy (World Bank 1994; Golub 2005). The development donors' governance agenda won widespread support and grew more explicit in the late 1990s and 2000s as corruption came to the forefront of aid rhetoric, and the UN agencies and World Bank converged toward strategies that often blend 1980s vintage market liberalization with poverty and human development programs (Stern 2002; UNDP 2005).

This neat periodization, of course, is a historical typology. New initiatives in development rarely replace the old; rather the initiatives accumulate to create a mixed and confused set of strategies. The 1970s emphasis on basic human needs was appended to the drive for economic growth, and although the neoliberal revolution moved basic needs from the theoretical center of development, donors continued to fund (and showcase) direct antipoverty and human development programs. The result is a widely varied set of development approaches that give lip service to government initiative in the development process but fund programs based on a diverse set of donor agencies' mandates, priorities, and cultures.

Moreover, coordination among donors is strong but not complete. The so-called Washington Consensus of the 1980s and 1990s was resisted by a minority of donors that favored state-led programs (Japan) or employment and human services (Netherlands and the Scandinavian countries). The United Nations Children's Fund (UNICEF) fought a rear-guard battle against orthodox structural adjustment in the 1980s with its "Adjustment with a Human Face" theme, and UNDP adopted a new strategy in the 1990s, publishing the annual Human Development Reports and developing and promoting indices of human development that challenged GDP growth as an indicator of a society's development status. In 2000, UNDP began to explicitly link its human development to human rights, arguing that "human development is essential for realizing human rights, and human rights are essential for full human development" (UNDP 2000, 2).

UNDP has played a further role as interpreter of important theoretical work on the human rights–development nexus. The works of Amartya Sen, Martha Nussbaum, and Thomas Pogge have provided a basis in the theory of entitlements, human capabilities, and human rights responsibilities, and UNDP has drawn on these and encouraged them, featuring Nussbaum's and Sen's writings in their *Human Development Report* background papers and serving as a bridge between theory and development practice. Sen's re-examination of the workings of markets emphasizes the concept of entitlements and the central roles that governments play in shaping economic institutions. Political freedoms, the flow of information, and lively "public action" play a central role, Sen shows, in creating the conditions under which government protects the entitlements of vulnerable groups in society (Sen and Drèze 1989; Sen 2000). Nussbaum's work, particularly *Women and Human Development*, proposes a philosophical basis for development policy that has proven attractive to thinkers in the UN system. By emphasizing government's obligation to create conditions that preserve human functioning above minimum levels, Nussbaum, although preferring "capabilities" to rights, provides an intellectual framework for an approach to development that starts from the inalienable rights of individuals and obligations of governments.

These intellectual challenges to conventional thinking about development have lent support and legitimacy to efforts to link development more closely with human rights. More important in explaining the movement toward rights-based approaches, though, are the political, moral, and organizational challenges discussed in the section that follows.

Crisis of Development, Promise of Human Rights

By the late 1990s, the development aid enterprise faced a crisis both of substance and of image, felt most acutely by leading NGOs and the donors most concerned with social welfare outcomes. Four critical issues capture the dimensions of the crisis: the continuing growth of inequality and social exclusion in most low-income countries; the desire by many NGOs to challenge prevailing neoliberal economic norms in the field; the deeply compromised independence of NGOs as participants in civil society; and the weakness of accountability by development programs and donors to those they purport to serve. Collectively, these changes and the pressures they created for international development NGOs—financial, moral, political, and intellectual—are the motives that drive NGOs' strategic choices to adopt human rights–based approaches.

POVERTY AND INEQUALITY

The increasing intensity and complexity of poverty and global inequality is the most significant of the global factors driving some NGOs to find ways to increase the impact of their programming and to influence trade, finance, and other policies more decisively. The UN-sponsored Millennium Development Goals and Campaign and the development NGO–led "One" campaign against global poverty have helped bring poverty reduction back to the center of official development discourse, emphasizing quick impact interventions in health education, water, and sanitation. But the extent and severity of global poverty, outside of rapidly growing China, continued to worsen in the late 1990s and the first years of the new millennium. Even in the measured language of the 2006 UN report on the Decade for the Eradication of Poverty (1997–2006), the progress "has been mixed" (United Nations Economic and Social Council 2005, 12). "[A]t the global level" the incidence of extreme poverty declined by 118 million persons, but in one country, China, 165 million people were, statistically speaking, lifted out of poverty. On balance, then, except in China's superheated new industrial economy, "all other regions have experienced setbacks since 1990," not only in Africa but in Latin America, Europe, and Central Asia as well (United Nations Economic and Social Council 2005, 13).

In the context of this persistent and growing poverty, both NGOs and official agencies have searched for a magic bullet, a change in outlook and strategy that would restore development's luster in the public eye and make a rapid and sustainable difference for 1.2 billion people living in extreme poverty. The Oxfam agencies, for example, according to Oxfam America's president, wanted a new, dynamic approach to poverty that "defines poverty as social exclusion" and identifies the "critical exclusionary mechanism," rather than resource deficits (Offenheiser and Holcombe 2003). DFID similarly argues that human rights–based development recasts poverty as a result of exclusion and discrimination, not simply a "lack of resources" (2000, 13), and Sida (2001) claims that the improved ability to analyze poverty and its causes is the most important benefit of its rights and democracy approach.

ActionAid's 2005–2010 action plan highlights the "unacceptable truth that poverty remains deeply entrenched around the globe" and that the "gap between rich and poor communities and nations is . . . widening." Acting on "our deepening understanding of the causes of poverty and injustice," it adopts a "Rights to End Poverty" strategy (ActionAid 2005, 2–3).

CHALLENGING THE MARKET-DRIVEN DEVELOPMENT PARADIGM

If the urgency of securing global commitments to eradicate poverty is the principal factor motivating development NGOs to embrace rights-based approaches, resistance to the dominance of free-market ideology is nearly as important. While many agencies seek to reconcile rapid privatization and free-market strategies with poverty reduction, the rights-based approach subordinates free markets to the legal and moral claims to a standard of material well-being. The development paradigm of the early twenty-first century has updated the so-called Washington Consensus, assigning more importance to the open and efficient management of state agencies and returning poverty to the center of the rhetoric of development. The faith of 1980s free-market proponents confronted social, political, and institutional realities in the 1980s and 1990s, and market-driven development now includes modifiers such as broadly based, sustainable, and "pro-poor."

But while the discourse of human development highlights poverty, the increasingly strong link between development assistance and private sector investment, and the hyperspeed of global currency and financial markets, remain the dominant factors in shaping aid strategies for global development. The rapid growth of transnational corporate activity and influence, and the halting efforts to create a system of rules and governance for finance, development, and trade have dramatically narrowed the real policy choices available to poor-country governments (Wade 2003). The integration of most major aid donors with these trade and finance rules means that a development path that does not offer free rein to transnational corporations will not find favor or support from major donors. In productive sectors such as agriculture, forestry, and mining—as in social and public services such as water, sanitation, and health care—aid donors have systematically integrated their grants and loans with corporate investments and contracting.

Largely as a result of this shift toward aid as a stimulus to privatization and a catalyst for private investment, international NGOs in development are giving greater weight to research, advocacy, advice, and technical assistance related to trade and investment strategies and negotiations (Lindenberg and Bryant 2001). For NGOs committed to this sort of development work, a human rights framework provides a legal and normative counterweight to the powerful neoliberal norms. In their advocacy on trade rules and HIV/AIDS, for example, both Doctors Without Borders (MSF) and Oxfam rely heavily on the assertion that access to care for HIV-infected patients is an essential component of the internationally recognized human right to health care ('t Hoen 2000; Health GAP 2006; Oxfam International 2002b). The slogan for Oxfam's working paper series on the pharmaceutical industry, "The right to medicines, or the right to profit from medicines?" captures the use of human rights as counterleverage.

THE COMPROMISED INDEPENDENCE OF NGOs
A third source of interest in the rights-based approach is the independence of NGOs themselves. As international NGOs have been drawn deeper into an aid system dominated by donors and major industrial governments, their identity as independent, "voluntary," or even "nongovernmental" is sometimes called into question. Dependence on the aid industry is an issue for NGOs worldwide (Hulme and Edwards 1997), but it may be most keenly felt in the United States, particularly in politically charged conflict situations. In 2003, USAID administrator Andrew Natsios urged NGOs working in Iraq to recognize that they, like contractors, are "arms of the U.S. government" and threatened that if NGOs did not demonstrate stronger ties to U.S. foreign policy, he would find other partners (Natsios 2003). His remarks reinforced then secretary of state Colin Powell's characterization of NGOs as "force multipliers" for the U.S. government (Stoddard 2003).

Human rights–based approaches are in part an urgent attempt to define and articulate credible roles and identities that reassert NGO independence and thus shore up NGOs' moral authority and power. Rights-based approaches offer two sources of renewed identity and independence for international development NGOs: a commitment to principles and standards that are enshrined in international agreements, and the possibility of new forms of solidarity with social movements, NGOs, and citizens' organizations in poor countries.

ACCOUNTABILITY

Finally, human rights offers the potential for clarity in international NGOs' world of complex and competing accountability claims. Development is an enterprise without a legal or moral anchor. Humanitarian practice has a basis in soft law and treaties (Forsythe 2005), and human rights has standards and principles that are enshrined in international treaties, but development cooperation is governed by fashion, donors' wishes, negotiated agreements between parties, and the hand of the market. The existence of standards of good professional practice, or standards of conduct among international NGOs such as those maintained by the U.S. umbrella agency InterAction, the British association BOND, and other associations of national NGOs (Jordan 2005), does not change the fact that development as an enterprise is pinned to high hopes and to the compassion and solidarity of dedicated professionals, without binding standards to give it direction or to establish accountability.

International development NGOs are particularly plagued by ambiguous and confused lines of accountability. Although strong relationships to local NGOs and community-based organizations are touted as strengths of international development NGOs (Fowler 1997; Lewis 2001), donors and governments exert the most powerful and structured claims through reporting requirements, contracts, and legal and regulatory powers. Demands for greater NGO accountability are wide-ranging, from routine demands for financial accountability and calls for accountability to the people and communities affected by their programs (Ebrahim 2005; Jordan and Van Tuijl 2006), to questions about international NGOs' legitimacy as political actors (Nelson 1997; Edwards 2000; Roe 1995; Bob 2005).

In principle, embracing human rights standards would clarify the accountability; NGOs that accept human rights as binding standards for their work have a clear basis for choosing program priorities and strategies, and they make themselves accountable to those standards. They have stronger grounds for insisting that governmental donors do the same, respecting human rights as development's central goal, regardless of the individual donor's other priorities.

How effectively accountability to these standards and principles can be enforced in making economic and social policy is a subject of much debate, and the rapidly growing experience with building legal and political accountability to ESC rights is discussed in chapters 2 and 4. But limited legal precedent and relatively weak international institutions for enforcing ESC rights are not barriers to the adoption of human rights standards as the basis for organizational accountability and programmatic priority setting by international development NGOs. Legal enforcement of economic and social rights is not central to most development agency strategies, and despite the imprecision of some standards bemoaned by some human rights practitioners, they create standards that are altogether absent from development practice. Moreover, creating measurable targets and monitoring systems is a strength of development practice.

Development Agencies and the Tentative Embrace of Rights-Based Development

To assess how development agencies are implementing rights-based approaches, we have created a three-part typology of the methods being employed to implement rights-based approaches. The typology emphasizes three characteristics of the international NGO's implementation: how public and visible; how system-wide; and how clearly and specifically rooted in internationally recognized human rights standards and principles. By highlighting the varied choices that agencies have made, the typology allows us to see how selective and varied the rights-based approach remains in implementation.

A TYPOLOGY

To highlight the key points of difference in methods of implementing rights-based approaches, consider the three dimensions of this typology:

Public and visible: Rhetorical affirmation of human rights as the basis for programming and advocacy is significant, as mission statements, fundraising appeals, and slogans can all be articulated in terms of meeting universal obligations rather than solely responding to human needs. Communicating rights-based programming to donors and supporters accustomed to the discourse of needs and poverty reduction is a critical challenge.

Each NGO's strategic choices about standards, advocacy, service delivery, and the public profile of its rights-based work is also an exercise in positioning with respect to donors, members, southern partners and social movements, and other constituencies.

System-wide: Organizations have diverse styles of implementation, especially organizations whose work is geographically dispersed and functionally varied. Some invoke human rights principles primarily in their work on specific issues; Christian Aid's work on *dalits* or untouchables in India is an example, as is Irish Cortaid's work with ethnic minorities (Harris-Curtis, Marleyn, and Bakewell 2005). Neither of these organizations has embraced a human rights–based approach more broadly, and we focus primarily on international NGOs that have a stated commitment to a broader human rights approach. We ask how universally the rights-based approach is implemented, across country programs or regional lines, as well as across divides between advocacy, service delivery, and education. Making this assessment is complex. ActionAid, for example, has made a global commitment to a human rights–based approach, but features a strongly decentralized country-based planning and programming structure.

Among the features we assess in asking how systemic is implementation are:

- *Analysis and assessment* of progress by governments toward fulfilling rights, using international human rights standards as the basis to analyze causes of poverty and design possible interventions, as well as to judge the impact of aid donors and of corporate conduct, is a second function of human rights standards.

- *Advocacy* becomes a higher priority for development NGOs under a rights-based approach. When states have primary responsibility for fulfilling human rights to food, housing, health, and education, NGOs and donors have to take the state's capacities and policies seriously.

- *Human rights education, motivation, and empowerment* is an option in every aspect of NGOs' work, from fundraising in the industrial countries to service delivery, but has not been widely embraced by development agencies.

- *Program design and implementation* is the most ambiguous area, and agencies have not systematically worked out what a rights-based approach means for programming priorities, for funding allocations by country, or for program design.

- *Rootedness in human rights standards, principles, and methods:* How specifically and clearly does the NGO refer to human rights standards and principles (nondiscrimination, universality, etc.), and to what extent does it employ any traditional human rights methods, such as documentation and reporting, human rights education, or litigation?

Looking across these functions of the rights-based approach, it becomes clear that what is occurring is not a transformation of development NGOs by a human rights–based methodology, but the shaping and adaptation of aspects of the rights-based approach to fit individual organizations' own images.

The rights-based approach provides principles, but not a blueprint, and NGOs are shaping their own answers to fundamental choices between a violations, promotion, or service delivery approach; between international or local advocacy; between explicit reference to standards and a broader human rights ethos; and between a public and visible embrace of human rights and a quiet, stealth approach.

The geographical and organizational breadth of international development NGOs, and the relative decentralization of programmatic decision making in many of them, make organizational generalizations problematic. We offer a set of illustrative programs and initiatives taken by four of the leading adherents of the rights-based approach, portraying broad organizational tendencies and the possibilities and limitations of the present embrace of rights-based approaches. None of the options is exclusive of the others, but a clear pattern of preference for promotion approaches is taking shape among development agencies at all levels.

PUBLIC ADVOCACY, GLOBAL VISION

Oxfam bases its rights-based approach on the agreement among all members of the Oxfam family, outlined in a strategic plan titled *Towards Global Equity*. While all of the thirteen national Oxfams carry out emergency relief and development assistance projects, the clear focus of Oxfam's implementation of a rights-based approach is in its advocacy and campaigning work on global rules and institutions.

Oxfam's rights framework is to some extent self-defined, consisting of five categories of rights to which Oxfam commits itself: the right to a sustainable livelihood, to basic social services, to life and security, to be heard, and to equity (Oxfam International 2002a). Individual Oxfam affiliates identify priority areas for their work; in 2002 Oxfam GB outlined an agenda focused on HIV/AIDS, conflict, corruption, and migration and refugees, and its Strategic Plan for 2003–04 through 2005–06 added emphases on livelihood, education, and gender.

In operational terms, Oxfam identifies six implications of the rights-based approach, the broadest and most concrete of standards by any of the new rights-based approach agencies. Participants in its international training workshops are instructed that a rights-based approach means:

- Program goals focus on people and their rights
- Work with other agencies toward shared rights-based goals
- Concentrate on the worst rights violations and the most vulnerable, marginalized people
- Strengthen accountability of duty bearers for human rights
- Support people's efforts to demand their rights
- Fight discrimination and promote equality and inclusion of all people in development policy and initiatives (Theis 2003).

Concretely, this has primarily meant global-level advocacy and grant making to local partner organizations in the poor countries.

Oxfam's approach to rights-based development work builds on the organization's experience as a campaigning NGO working at the international level. Through campaigning work in the 1990s on themes including debt and fair trade and the creation of an Oxfam International office in Washington to advocate at the UN and international financial institutions, Oxfam established itself as the preeminent advocacy organization on development policy issues.

The links between Oxfam's international advocacy agenda and its embrace of human rights are uneven. All issues on the agenda are consistent with the five aims, but only occasionally is there a specific reference to human rights standards and their implications. The agenda has been dominated by trade issues related to WTO rules and Oxfam's "make trade fair" theme, access to medicines and care for HIV/AIDS patients, education for girls, and the One Campaign, which is in turn linked to the antipoverty theme of the Millennium Development Goals. The series of briefing papers on major pharmaceutical companies is one of the most clearly human rights–focused: the series title is "the right to medicines, or the right to profit from medicines" (Oxfam International 2002b).

Oxfam's grant-making and local-capacity-building programs also experienced a shift toward explicit human rights organizations as partners, toward organizations with an emphasis on social and economic policy advocacy, or toward organizations with historic ties to civil liberties and human rights work. This would all be evidence of movement toward implementing a human rights–based approach.

Samples of grants to new organizational partners, before and after the rights-based approach, show that new partner organizations worldwide and in the Latin American/Caribbean region were more likely to directly address human rights issues, use human rights language and concepts in written materials, and be active in human rights–related partnerships and network relationships (Doperak and Szabo 2003; Oxfam America 2002).

The Oxfam family's embrace of human rights approaches has been highly public. Publications discuss Oxfam's work in terms of rights fulfillment, often alongside the language of needs and opportunities.

Oxfam America's president has coauthored a paper on the issues involved in implementing a rights-based approach at Oxfam (Offenheiser and Holcombe 2003); Oxfam International made (former) UN high commissioner for human rights Mary Robinson honorary chair of its board and prominently features her statements on Oxfam's behalf in publications.

CARE: STEALTH IMPLEMENTATION OF LOCAL SERVICE DELIVERY METHODS

CARE adopted a rights-based approach that "deliberately and explicitly focuses on people achieving the minimum conditions for living with dignity (i.e., achieving their human rights). It does so by exposing the roots of vulnerability and marginalization, and expanding the range of responses" (Picard 2003, 2).

CARE International, like the Oxfam groups, is organized as an international federation of national CARE affiliates. Unlike Oxfam, CARE's adoption of a rights-based approach is surprising in that policy advocacy has not been as large a part of CARE's historic work or image, and CARE was not known for partnerships with politicized local and national civil society organizations. More surprising, perhaps, is that the initiative came first from CARE-USA. CARE-USA relies substantially on the U.S. Agency for International Development for emergency and development funds, and USAID's lack of enthusiasm for economic and social rights likely helps to explain the relatively low profile that the rights-based initiative has had at CARE.

Yet CARE's planning and articulation of its rights-based approach, and its analysis of the organizational implications, are thorough and insightful. Staff members assigned to the human rights initiative have developed and carried out one-day introductory training sessions for CARE staff and have facilitated discussions of further likely organizational changes (CARE 2005).

CARE links implementation of its rights-based approach to its Household Livelihood Security methodology for programs in rural areas, tying the new initiative to a well-established methodology with broad support among CARE workers and recognition among other practitioners (Ambler 2002). CARE has introduced the human rights approach through project-specific and country pilot operations and coordinates the work of interested country programs through a rights-based approach reference group that meets annually to discuss pilot efforts and analyze new conceptual tools such as "power analysis" and "causal responsibility analysis" that are designed to help the staff use human rights standards and principles to discover the underlying causes of poverty (Picard 2003, 4).

CARE has also produced a thorough set of case studies probing the effects of its rights-based approach (Rand 2002). The review of five case studies examines projects in civil society promotion and livelihood security that have employed rights-based methods, drawing both specific conclusions for projects as well as organization-wide lessons for management and policy.

CARE offers some of the clearest examples of how an agency can ground situation analysis and the monitoring of development projects in human rights principles and standards. A country study of Burundi, for example, shows how CARE national staffers used analysis of patterns of discrimination against the Batwa minority, and their "systematic marginalization," to analyze chronic poverty and devise interventions that address its causes (CARE International 2003, 30–37).

In Africa, several CARE projects apply an analysis of nondiscrimination to situations in which legal, social, customary, and other rules and institutions affect the opportunities of excluded groups to gain access to important institutions or services. CARE's "rights-based monitoring tool" for Malawi, for example, is anchored in the analysis of discrimination to understand the limited access of poor rural households to land, credit, and agricultural inputs (Goulden and Glyde 2004); declining livelihoods in Malawi and its impact on the poor; and the differential impact of HIV/AIDS on poor households.

In general, rigorous attention to nondiscrimination moves development planners from asking whether a given program or service will "reach" intended beneficiaries to asking whether it counters existing discriminatory tendencies, fosters institutions and policies that systemically attack discriminatory practices, and creates models for accessibility and nondiscriminatory extension of benefits, services, and opportunities. Nondiscrimination as an analytic approach forces agencies to focus not only on the fact of deprivation, but on its social, legal, political, and institutional causes.

CARE's strategy for rights-based policy advocacy has focused on assistance and capacity building for advocacy among its African NGO partners. The SCAPE program (Strengthening Capacities for Transforming Relationships and Exercising Rights) has trained and supported local advocates across sub-Saharan Africa (CARE 2006).

Policy advocacy has not been a high priority historically at CARE, and its modest efforts have focused on aid policy and funding. But CARE staff members see the rights-based strategy as requiring the organization to devote resources to advocacy that reinforces governments' and international agencies' obligations and capacities to fulfill (especially) economic and social rights.

The Swedish national agency Sida—although not an NGO—shares CARE's emphasis on human rights as a means of better analyzing the causes of poverty. Indeed, Sida's "Democracy and Human Rights" approach aspires to analyze development issues including poverty and inequality through a human rights lens (2001). Sida considers the Country Development Strategy Process the key stage in implementing this approach (Johnston 2000, 42), and a review of one early country analysis, for Zambia, shows a concerted effort to conceptualize and analyze poverty and social policy issues in terms of human rights (Sida 2003, 1017). This is markedly different from the previous Zambia country document, where "human rights" referred almost exclusively to civil and political rights and social policy was analyzed without reference to rights (Sida 1998b, 17–22). The 2003 country analysis features sustained analysis of patterns of discrimination but little discussion of power structures.

CHILDREN'S RIGHTS PROMOTION AT SAVE THE CHILDREN

Founded in London in 1919, Save the Children (STC) responded to the plight of World War I orphans by calling for worldwide safeguards for children and for recognition of children's rights. Save the

Children now includes thirty national affiliates working in one hundred countries, and its work to improve the lives of children and their communities addresses HIV/AIDS, education, armed conflicts and disasters, children exploitation and abuse, and other children's rights. The organization receives support from donor organizations and from individual contributors, and it raised US$430 million in 2001 (International Save the Children Alliance 2001).

STC Sweden embraces the rights-based approach, working with like-minded STC members, such as STC UK, to develop operational tools for children's rights programming. Save the Children argues that adopting a rights-based approach improves its traditional program work by emphasizing long-term goals, using internationally accepted standards to measure progress, and embracing a legal framework that identifies the responsibilities of governments, donors, the private sector, communities, and individuals. It incorporates principles such as participation, nondiscrimination, and poverty eradication into a unified, rights-based approach (International Save the Children Alliance 2002).

STC Sweden bases its development work rigorously on international human rights laws, standards, and values. It employs an analytical framework that focuses at the national level on the adequacy of protection for the rights of children, emphasizing four human rights principles: child participation, nondiscrimination, accountability, and the principle of "best interest of the child."

A list of program areas such as children in armed conflict and disaster and children's right to be heard and to participate serves as a programming framework from which regional and country offices are to choose priorities in creating national strategies.[1] Organization policies, objectives, strategies, and implementation methods are spelled out for each program area, providing comprehensive strategy papers and emphasizing four broad methodologies: research and analysis; direct material support; knowledge dissemination and capacity building; advocacy and awareness raising (Save the Children Sweden 2001).

In addition to the "program area" framework, STC Sweden has worked with other STC members to develop a programming tool, "Child Rights Programming" (CRP). CRP is the most crucial component of STC's rights-based approach, and it refers to "using the Principles of Child Rights to Plan, Manage, Implement and Monitor Programmes with the Overall goal of strengthening the rights of the child as defined in International Law" (International Save the Children Alliance 2002, 23).

It is difficult to point to dramatic changes in STC because of its historic commitments to children's human rights. That longstanding commitment and its focus on a single rights-bearing group facilitate the task of implementing the rights-based approach, and it has chosen a decentralized approach that introduces and encourages innovation in its country offices. The results are uneven implementation. Child Rights Programming is "marginalized" in some country programs, particularly those that emphasize direct assistance, but innovation and informal pilot program experience is shared through network-wide meetings on CRP.

STC Sweden also emphasizes advocacy work, lobbying several UN bodies and European governments and the European Union. In other countries, advocacy is carried out by urban-based civil society organizations with which STC Sweden works. Like most international development NGOs, STC does not directly lobby southern governments, opting for advocacy–capacity building of local activist organizations. Activism for STC Sweden involves public campaigning, media work, and popular mobilization in defense of the rights of poor and marginalized people (Theis 2003). STC Sweden has invested heavily in human rights education (Theis 2003) as a means of encouraging longer-term changes through deeper awareness in civil societies of children's rights and human rights mechanisms.

ACTIONAID'S LOCAL RIGHTS-BASED ADVOCACY

ActionAid's rights-based approach, adopted as a global policy in 2006, is shaped by the agency's highly decentralized structure and longstanding commitment to local advocacy work. The experience of ActionAid India (AAI) illustrates the agency's politically engaged, locally focused approach to rights-based development. The organization has no central definition or prescription of what a rights-based approach means operationally. National ActionAid organizations have considerable discretion in specifying the implications of the rights-based approach for their programmatic work.

ActionAid India's (2006) mission, to restore rights of poor and marginalized people by working with organizations of such people, requires that rights, which "may be constitutional, moral and/or legal entitlements," protect all people. Targeting poor and marginalized groups, AAI works with local organizations and social movements "who have the knowledge and enjoy the confidence of the communities we work with."

Under the slogan "Rights First!" AAI is committed to helping challenge government policy and win the implementation of legal and policy protections for the full range of human rights. In 2001, the Indian Supreme Court ordered measures taken to strengthen food security. An AAI initiative to investigate and document "irregularity and pilferage" in one grain distribution program uncovered local arrangements that were systematically denying food to families belonging to the Sahariya tribal group and profiting from the resale of food. Local investigations and petitions by AAI network partners led to a government investigation and a report to the Supreme Court. The results in 2006 included 37,492 new ration cards issued to Sahariya families and the abolition of the contracting system that allowed diversion schemes to function (Pattnaik and Sharma 2006).

While much of the dynamism of ActionAid's rights-based approach originates in the organization's national programs, it has created an organization-wide monitoring system that is a distinctive feature of its approach. The Accountability, Learning and Planning System (ALPS), introduced with the rights-based approach in 2000, aims to infuse human rights principles into its system for monitoring and assessing all its program work. From the human rights perspective, ALPS's distinguishing feature is the intensive involvement of community, local partner organizations, and poor people themselves in the assessment of ActionAid's work (Guijt 2004).

As with the other three NGOs reviewed in table 3.1, ActionAid's mandate and organizational characteristics shape the distinctive rights-based approach it has adopted.

Table 3.1 Four International Development NGOs' Implementation of Rights-Based Approaches

	OXFAM	ACTIONAID	CARE	SAVE THE CHILDREN
Public and visible	High	High	Low	High
System-wide	Strongest in global-level advocacy; also apparent in grant-making to local NGOs and movements.	Decentralized; strongest at national level programming and advocacy.	Pilot programs; strong reflection, research, and training; African examples dominate.	Embraces "human rights programming," attempts diffusion across global federation. Sweden and UK among strongest.
Rooted in human rights standards, principles, & methods	"Five Aims" identify areas of rights drawn from international standards.	Global: "Rights to End Poverty" India: "rights first" approach recognizes constitutional, legal, and moral entitlements rooted in international human rights.	Strong use of human rights principles, especially non-discrimination, in analytical work.	Focus on children allows STC to make CRC the centerpiece of organizational mission. Rigorous reference to standards and principles from CRC.

Human Rights and the Millennium Development Goals

Launched in 2000, the Millennium Development Goals (MDGs) sparked an unusual show of united purpose among official donors.[2] The eight goals with eighteen standards and forty-eight benchmarks and indicators call for reductions in poverty, malnutrition, illiteracy, child mortality, gender discrimination, and other indicators of human development from 1990 levels to new levels by 2015. They are the centerpiece of a research, publicity, and education campaign to build donor support for human development programs.

The MDGs aim to motivate and mobilize support from major donor countries and their citizens by demonstrating the capacity of "development" to accomplish some real and important tasks. They represent much of what development cooperation does best: defining goals, objectives, and benchmarks and monitoring and measuring progress toward them. Development agencies have financed important successes in this way, advancing public health and immunization coverage in the 1980s, for example, in ways that advanced life expectancy and reduced child and infant mortality—at least until the effects of the AIDS pandemic became severe in the 1990s.

But the MDGs call on the donors only to endorse and promote another in a series of donor-announced initiatives. They include no accountability mechanisms for the rich countries; they essentially ignore access to land, employment, and credit, investing in "quick win" strategies such as immunizations, mosquito nets, and education subsidies.

The practices of global goal setting and pledging by donors are firmly entrenched in development practice. Compared to human rights–driven policy, it is hard not to see the MDGs as a watered-down replacement in which goals replace rights and generosity replaces obligations.

Human rights–based approaches insist on analysis of the *causes* of poverty and of the deprivations, inequality, and violations of rights that accompany it; the MDGs are output indicators that aim for progress in some of the worst *symptoms* of poverty. Both in principle and in practice, human rights approaches to social and economic policy have involved tracing the social, economic, political, and other causes of rights deprivation. CARE, Sida, ActionAid, and others affirm that one of the principal advantages afforded by a human rights framework is a structured means of tracing the often multiple causes of poverty, social exclusion, and denial of any specific right.

The MDGs, on the other hand, create incentives that favor quick impact over complex social systems. The MDGs' "quick wins" strategy, as outlined in the 2005 UN report on investing to advance the MDGs, funds "high potential, short-term impact" initiatives that can yield "breathtaking results within three or fewer years" and "start countries on the path to the Goals." These quick-impact measures include, for example, financing mosquito bed nets for malaria protection, MDG "villages," immunizations, school meals, and water purification devices. Investments of this kind have two kinds of payoff in MDG terms: they begin to drive down the key indicators for the goals, and they offer the prospect of quick impact that can mobilize donors' aid funds.

In pragmatic terms, this is the advantage of the MDGs: the goals establish benchmarks with attainable levels of progress, and they tend to rely on interventions (mosquito nets for malaria, nutrition supplementation) that can be accomplished without even attempting to address the thorny social and political causes of inequality and deprivation.

But embracing this strategy for a global antipoverty initiative means de-emphasizing other strategies. Of the structural factors accounting for poverty and wealth in poor countries—access to land, labor, wages, credit, and entrepreneurial opportunity—none is touched upon by the MDGs. The only attention given to discrimination is in the call for eliminating disparities between boys' and girls' school enrollment rates.

Does it matter? How consequential is the difference between rights and goals?

First, rights *belong* to individuals, while goals *refer* to individuals but belong to the governments and international agencies that set them.

Agreement among governments that poverty or maternal mortality should be reduced by half, for example, does not give any particular poor person or expectant mother the right of access to land, food, prenatal care, or other economic or social good, without discrimination, that she needs. When government services are maldistributed or inadequate, or when land or credit is distributed in a discriminatory manner, the existence of a goal does not give any citizen the legal or political grounds on which to challenge existing policy and press for change. Neither human rights standards nor development goals are self-enforcing, of course, and the record of enforceability of economic and social human rights is only now growing. But in principle, human rights afford a legal and political leverage and a source of accountability that is absent or vastly weaker with goals.

It should not be surprising that while ESC rights have become an important moral, legal, and political framework for social movements calling for improved AIDS treatment or access to water or land (see chapter 4), the MDGs have gained little attention from such movements (Nelson 2007). Paradoxically, internationally recognized human rights to economic and social goods, framed in treaties to which states are legally bound, have become the favored vehicle for social movement mobilization, while many states opt to frame objectives in terms of nonbinding, essentially voluntary goals.

The United Nations system, too, has become more comfortable framing development objectives as goals rather than as human rights. It appeared in 2001 that the UN system was moving toward a systematic embrace of human rights as the framework for social and economic work. But by 2007, the profile of human rights in the public materials and websites of UNICEF and UNDP had receded in favor of a united push for the MDGs. The comment from the human rights movement has been muted. Philip Alston, advisor on the MDGs to the high commissioner for human rights, published what might be expected to be an authoritative comment in a 2004 *Human Rights Quarterly* article, and he is careful to emphasize and encourage the hoped-for synergies between the MDGs and rights-based approaches to development.

Alston may be proven correct, but if this is to come to pass it will require a much stronger, more concerted effort than is now visible to link the MDGs to the standards, principles, and power of human rights and to encourage the power that human rights standards should afford to people living in the indignity of extreme poverty.

Durability and Limits, Constraints and Resistance

Is this ambivalence within the United Nations a symptom of a general lack of substantive change by the official and nongovernmental agencies embracing human rights–based development? Skeptics have argued that the rush to adopt rights-based approaches is an expression of donors' continuing effort to win greater legitimacy for the development enterprise. Donors may be doing little more, as Uvin (2002, 1–2) suggests, than attempting to occupy the moral "high ground" by "incorporating human rights terminology into development discourse," a rhetorical gesture that need not involve substantive changes in the policies, projects, and programs they promote.

Skepticism is entirely appropriate in light of the history of development fashions, and to reach a more definitive understanding of what development agencies are doing with the rights-based approach, agencies and those who monitor them need to use a set of standards and methods that would provide convincing evidence of genuine, substantive changes driven by human rights–based approaches. What changes are apparent in organizational systems, such as management and training, funding, and cooperative partnerships, to show in the longer term that fundamental change is in process?

What course the embrace of human rights will take in the development field is difficult to anticipate. To date it has been selective, irregular, and sometimes frustrating to those who advocate a thorough transformation. There are reasons, both inherent to human rights and social policy themselves, and specific to the politics of the development field, to think that impact in the development sector will continue to be somewhat limited.

Foremost among these is the relative reluctance to exercise power in a forthright, direct manner. ActionAid is the most prominent exception to this aversion to power, as the agency directly affirms its objective of increasing the power available to poor people's organizations and others with whom it works. Other agencies—Oxfam and MSF, for example—while not engaging in a discourse of power, do position themselves to be able to use human rights principles to give greater force to their demands. But until development NGOs become more comfortable with the highly politicized world of social movements, their embrace of human rights principles will have less than resounding impact.

The organizational and international politics of the development field also seem likely to limit the impact of human rights–based approaches. Resistance from some donors constitutes the most obvious limit. CARE staff members specializing in developing and promoting its rights-based approach acknowledge that the organization's donors, particularly government agencies including USAID, have some hesitations about the emphasis on rights that will have to be overcome or dealt with (Bode et al. 2005).

How independently can international NGOs in the development field be expected to act? Development NGOs are often lumped in an amorphous, wide-ranging collective referred to as "global civil society" (e.g., in Anheier, Glasius, and Kaldor 2004; Salamon, Sokolowski, and Associates 2004). Tvedt (2002) and others have recently challenged the assumption that international development NGOs should be so treated and argue that they are better understood by grasping their place in the aid industry. Development NGOs, in this view, behave based on their structural position in the aid system, not the moral and independent position sometimes attributed to them.

Few international development NGOs have managed to build large-scale programs without bilateral and multilateral donors' support, and the largest of these donors—the U.S. and Japanese aid agencies and the World Bank—have little enthusiasm for a human rights–driven strategy.

The United Nations, which provided the principal source of initiative, has not proven to be a strong leader. Compromised and preoccupied by events relating to the September 11 attacks and the Iraq war and beset by constant criticism from the United States, its initiative has been weakened by the shift of focus to the Millennium Development Goals. However, UN agencies themselves have shone on a small scale: UNDP country programs such as that in Bosnia-Herzegovina, UNICEF's targeted programs on child nutrition and care of orphans, and the World Health Organization's use of human rights standards in professional standard setting work are examples.

What does the adoption and implementation of rights-based approaches by major international development NGOs imply for this debate? The evidence from the first years of implementation is mixed. Agencies that are relatively financially independent of the major donors—Oxfam, ActionAid—have been leaders in crafting rights-based approaches. But there appears to be room as well for independent innovation by agencies with strong ties to the flow of official aid money (CARE and Save the Children). Some NGO staff members argue that the U.S. affiliates of both these organizations are less advanced and less public in their embrace of human rights–based approaches (Harris-Curtis, Marleyn, and Bakewell 2005, 39).

Finally, fashion in development means that a new approach such as the rights-based approach can become a rigid form of orthodoxy, at least with some donors, discouraging innovation and creating resentments. Two leading movements among slum- and shack-dwellers, SPARC and the Slum Dwellers International network, have criticized the rights-based approach for dictating a one-strategy-fits-all approach. Respected housing activists Mitlin and Patel (2005) argue that the fashionability of rights-based approaches with some donors has made it difficult for SPARC and Slum Dwellers International to secure donor funding, because their preferred approach emphasizes local initiative and negotiated relationships with municipal and national government, not the assertion of rights and obligations.

The most serious danger is that NGOs' enthusiasm for rights-based development follows the pattern of other recent fashions, such as sustainable development, popular participation, and development "partnerships." Each of these was introduced as a reform with potential to transform the donor-driven system of development aid, but each has instead been adopted and thoroughly domesticated by aid donors, who have embraced the language while limiting the implications for it in practice. A similar dilution of human rights standards, the only widely accepted legal standards and political agreements for shaping national and global development, could be a great loss for global governance.

On the other hand, development may have a unique contribution to make to the advancement of economic and social rights. ESC rights practice in the human rights field, as we saw in chapter 2, has met with a variety of cautions and criticisms that ESC rights are not as readily enforceable, as clear and precise, or as immediately grasped by traditional human rights constituencies, as are civil and political rights. But these objections carry less weight in the development field, where NGOs are only occasionally concerned with litigating cases or issues and are more often drawing on ESC rights standards and principles for their political or analytic value.

Fashion plays a strong role in development, and the fashionability of rights-based approaches makes the durability of human rights–related innovations an important question, one that is difficult to answer at this early stage. It is not likely that international NGOs that have publicly embraced human rights–based approaches will turn away from them altogether. But, as at other times in the history of development, it would be entirely possible for NGOs and donors to quietly slide the rights-based approach onto the shelf that holds other slogans and principles for display to interested publics: sustainability, human development, gender empowerment, etc. This is not to say that individuals' commitments to these principles, and to the rights-based approach, are weak or insincere, but to suggest that organizational innovations may have transformative effects that are difficult to undo and incremental effects that are more easily eroded.

As long as rights-based methods remain one emphasis among others for a donor or an NGO, the cost to the organization of quietly de-emphasizing human rights at a later date is fairly small. The features to look for, therefore, in tracking the durability of the rights-based approach in an agency are skills, methods, staffing, and organizational changes that are difficult or costly (politically or financially) to undo.

Oxfam's adoption of a rights-based set of principles for its continuing global advocacy, for example, *could* be undone with little fanfare and little cost. Save the Children's long-term commitment would be more difficult (and unlikely) to reverse, with the organizational mission now pinned to the Convention on the Rights of the Child. CARE's situation is more difficult to discern. It has adopted its rights-based approach with little public fanfare, but in some country programs there has been extensive training and innovation. ActionAid has perhaps the most deeply entrenched rights-based approach of any of the mainstream development NGOs, with human rights standards and principles put at the center of strategies for social change and of planning processes with national partners.

The impetus that development NGOs see from advocacy alliances and campaigns, and from the handful of innovative hybrid organizations, are likely to be pivotal, and we will examine these alliances and organizations in detail in chapter 4.

Notes

1. The program areas are (a) exploitation and abuse of children; (b) children without sufficient family support; (c) children in armed conflict and disaster; (d) the child's rights to nondiscrimination; (e) the right to a good physical environment and good health; (f) the right to education; (g) children's rights to be heard and to participate; (h) the human rights of the child and child rights programming; (i) good governance in the best interest of the child; (j) a civil society for the rights of the child; and (k) knowledge management, capacity building, and rights-based program planning. Save the Children Sweden, Program Areas and Strategies, Stockholm: Save the Children Sweden n.d.
2. The section on the Millennium Development Goals draws heavily on Nelson (2007).

4

ALLIANCES AND HYBRIDS

I call upon governments to recognize the role of these
social movements in building a critical mass of
responsible citizens who help maintain the checks
and balances in society. On their part, civil society
should embrace not only their rights but their
responsibilities. Further, industry and global
institutions must appreciate that ensuring economic
justice, equity, and ecological integrity are of greater
value than profits at any cost.

—Wangari Maathai, Nobel Peace Prize Lecture, 2004

In chapter 1 we introduced the local and global trends that laid the
groundwork in the 1980s and early 1990s for the present human
rights–development convergence. Conflict over major infrastructure
projects and interactions around the UN-sponsored global conferences were reinforced by the facilitating roles of global social movements, especially the women's and indigenous peoples' movements,
bringing organizations and individuals into contact with each others'
methods and cultures.

These trends blossomed in the late 1990s into an extensive and
sometimes influential set of shared campaigns, alliances, and hybrid
organizations that reshaped the politics of NGO advocacy on social
and economic policy. In the most contentious social policy debates
since 2000—generic pharmaceuticals for HIV/AIDS, privatization of
water, corporate information disclosure, women's reproductive and
sexual rights—new alliances and new NGOs are bringing to bear
principles and methods from development and human rights and
forming alliances with social movements in an effort to assert new

125

political power to respond to new dimensions of poverty and social exclusion.

We review these trends here in four parts. Virtually every initiative profiled here can be traced to links formed during global conferences and during fights over major infrastructure projects in the 1980s and 1990s, so we begin by reviewing these conflicts, setting the stage for deeper integration. Second, we turn to cooperative shared issue campaigns; third, to deeper new rights campaigns on two issues, HIV/AIDS and water privatization, that decisively mix and exchange organizations' methodologies; and finally to the formation of hybrid organizations that integrate aspects of human rights and development practice in single NGOs.

These forms of shared action involve different levels and degrees of collaboration. In what we call collaborative issue campaigns—work on conflict diamonds, right to know, debt relief, child soldiers, and the "publish what you pay" campaign—activists from the two sectors work in cooperation, sometimes taking joint actions but oftentimes not, and rarely altering their methodologies. Convergent new rights alliances such as the work on HIV/AIDS and water privatization involve a crucial addition. Organizations clearly learn from each other's methods, adopt strategies and tactics across sector lines, and take joint initiatives that go beyond coordinated advocacy. Hybrid NGOs integrate the two sectors in an even more fundamental way, combining key features of human rights and development work in a single organization.

Together, these collaborative campaigns, convergent alliances, and hybrid organizations are the clearest indications of the new developments at the human rights–development nexus. First, they break down the sector divisions by sharing methods, rhetoric, agendas, strategies, and even individual staff members. Second, they openly articulate their objectives in terms of power in a way that distinguishes them from past international NGO initiatives in either sector, and that more closely resembles the posture of social movement organizations.

Few development NGOs make reference to power at all, preferring to emphasize opportunity, needs, and fairness even in their advocacy work. Most human rights NGOs assert that they are advocating for greater power or authority for human rights principles or standards. But these campaigns, alliances, and hybrids virtually all address power directly and adopt methods and strategies that call for greater power in rulemaking and greater authority over corporate and state actors.

We will see that each of these three forms of convergence—alliances, new rights campaigns, and hybrids—is deeply influenced by contact with community and national organizations in the poor countries and shaped by other changes in global systems, confirming the hypothesis advanced in chapter 1. The direct significance of these trends is for NGOs organized in the industrial countries. The lines that divide development and human rights have been much less significant among most NGOs in the poor countries, as multiple identities such as those of Kenya's Greenbelt Movement—development, environmental, women's rights, human rights NGO—are common.

Local and Global Cooperation Sets the Stage, 1980s–1990s

The local and global interactions around development projects and UN-sponsored global conferences produced three broad sets of results for environmental, development, and human rights advocates. Activists in each sector began to learn from the impact of the strategies employed in the others; international activists in all these sectors learned from their interaction with community groups and social movements in the poor countries, who often articulated their values and agendas in ways that crossed the northern activists' sector lines; and the interaction began to change expectations, especially in the human rights and development sectors, of the kind of work each carried out to advance its mission.

FIGHTING MAJOR INFRASTRUCTURE PROJECTS ACROSS THREE DECADES

Organized local resistance to certain major infrastructure projects has a long history, and major projects, which nearly always have implications for the distribution of land, water, energy, and wealth, have seldom been without controversy. Beginning in 1983, the Natural Resources Defense Council, Environmental Defense Fund, Sierra Club, and Friends of the Earth initiated a Multilateral Development Banks (MDB) project that brought these local debates to the global stage. Challenging World Bank financing of such projects (Rich 1994; Schwartzman 1986), they altered or blocked projects, which led to policy changes and new safeguards at the World Bank (Nelson 2002; Fox and Brown 1998). As international development and human rights NGOs engaged in these local conflicts, their objectives and strategies often differed, and their advocacy was seldom tightly coordinated.

International human rights NGO involvement has focused overwhelmingly on violations of civil and political rights in governments' treatment of villagers and demonstrators. A second current of human rights activism, smaller but growing, has called attention to the violations of ESC rights that accompany the loss of land and housing when river valleys are inundated. In early cases such as India's Narmada dams, this human rights engagement responded to allegations of civil and political rights violations. But by the mid-1990s, human rights, development, and environmental NGOs were monitoring disputed projects in a more coordinated and proactive way.

Development NGOs involved in campaigning sometimes signed on to statements and letters critical of notorious World Bank projects, including Narmada. But development NGOs' involvement is much more dependent on their physical presence and pre-existing working relationships with local organizations near the project site. The British NGO Christian Aid, for example, collaborated in the early 1990s with the Highland Church Action Group in Lesotho to monitor the massive Highland Water Project. The project, which dammed and reversed the flow of Lesotho's Senqu River, provoked local opposition, but Christian Aid, like most development NGOs, focused on ensuring adequate compensation and resettlement arrangements for villagers whose land was inundated. The story of international NGO involvement in the Sardar Sarovar Dam project on the Narmada River illustrates this parallel advocacy.

Sardar Sarovar Dam

Sardar Sarovar is the archetypal big dam project. Still a site of major organizing and controversy in 2007, it was planned in the 1950s and first financed with a $450 million World Bank loan in 1985. The international debate over Sardar Sarovar rose to an unprecedented level with the determined resistance of the Narmada Bachao Andolan (Save the Narmada, NBA), the stubborn and sometimes brutal insistence of the Indian government and Gujarat state that the project proceed, successful challenges within the World Bank primarily by international environmental NGOs, and the combination of social justice, environmental, and human rights themes in the debate.

Khagram's (2004) account focuses on the interactions among international actors, especially international environmental NGOs, and the community organizations in the Narmada Valley, especially the NBA, led by Medha Patkar. The agendas of the NBA, community organizations whose lands were to be flooded, and their international allies were varied and not always consistent. They included determined efforts to stop the dam, to reduce its height (and thus the area inundated), to compensate and relocate communities more adequately, to drive the World Bank from India, and to reform the World Bank's financing of infrastructure projects.

Systematic international support for Narmada Valley communities began in 1984 as Oxfam-UK and Survival International petitioned the British government and the World Bank for attention to the social and human impact of planned involuntary resettlements (Khagram 2004, 90–92). International organizing expanded in 1987 with the creation in Washington of the Narmada International Action Committee. Its membership, indicative of the network's outlook, included the NBA, international environmental NGOs (FOE Japan, Committee on Environment and Development, IRN, Probe International, Both Ends, and EDF); solidarity and cultural rights organizations [Action for World Solidarity, Rainforest Information Center, The Ecologist, Survival International, the Swedish NGO Svalorna (Swallows)]; and FIAN, the Hamburg-based network on the human right to food.

What began as a local campaign for land rights and against forced relocation was taken up in the international arena by environmental NGOs as an instance of World Bank–financed environmental destruction. Almost immediately, however, human and social impacts took center stage. Issues of cultural and indigenous rights were raised at first by NGOs such as Survival International and Cultural Survival, and the messages of the International Rivers Network, Environmental Defense Fund, Sierra Club, and Friends of the Earth rapidly took on added social, human, and human rights dimensions.

International human rights reporting began in earnest in the early 1990s. After a 1992 report by an ad hoc Narmada International Human Rights Panel and a 1993 Human Rights Campaign on Narmada, the Lawyers Committee for Human Rights (1993) released the first major international report. Human Rights Watch (HRW) and the Lawyers Committee remained involved, complementing intrepid human rights reporting by Indian NGOs, and environmental NGOs began routinely to report on human rights violations.

International human rights NGOs called attention to the ESC rights issues at Narmada only much later. The issue of evictions associated with development projects had long been discussed in UN settings, as in the Vienna Declaration of the 1993 Human Rights meetings (Vienna Declaration and Programme of Action 1993). COHRE, founded in 1994, monitored and reported on housing and tenure rights in the Narmada Valley beginning in 2000. COHRE newsletters and global updates on forced evictions prominently cite resettlements and forced evictions in the Narmada Valley to illustrate the global practice. Since 2000, while international human rights and environmental monitoring has continued to provide support and solidarity, many of the most significant incidents in the ongoing resistance have taken place in Indian state and national courts and administrative bodies (Lustig and Kingsbury 2006).

The growing integration of human rights, environmental, and development advocacy is not unique to large dam projects, as the recent history of petroleum exploration and extraction in Nigeria and Chad shows.

Chad-Cameroon Pipeline and Deepening Cooperation

The story of international activism in response to oil exploration and pipelines is a tale of the collision of the lifeblood of industrialized production and lifestyles with increasingly internationalized principles and norms of environmental and human rights practice. Oil-based economic development is a strategy with notorious economic, environmental, and social risks (Bannon and Collier 2003; Ross 2001), and controversy over oil, which created some of the flashpoints of international relations and development policy since 1980, has also been critical to accelerating cooperation and integration among the sectors of activism.

Two cases, from Nigeria and Chad, show how international advocacy on pipelines and their finance was transformed over fifteen years. In Nigeria's Niger River Valley, international NGO involvement grew largely in response to evidence of civil and political human rights abuses and of extensive and severe pollution caused by Shell Oil's operations. As the Nigerian government tightened controls over the activities of the Movement for the Survival of the Ogoni People (MOSOP), then arrested MOSOP leader Ken Saro-Wiwa in 1993, attention from environmental and human rights NGOs grew rapidly.

Saro-Wiwa's arrest and 1995 execution became a powerful symbolic link between human rights activism, environmental justice, and corporate (mis)conduct, and international outrage over the execution dramatically heightened international interest and support for local protests in the Niger Valley. It helped prepare international NGOs for prompt, concerted, and cooperative action in Chad and Cameroon, as the closely linked work of development, environment, and human rights NGOs on the Chad-Cameroon petroleum pipeline demonstrates.

In June 2000, the World Bank approved a loan to finance a pipeline by which oil extracted from Chad's Doba oilfield would be transported to port on the coast of Cameroon. The decision and the project were complex; petroleum reserves under the Chadian desert had the potential to transform the economy of one of the poorest countries of the planet, but the project was debated in the shadow of oil exploration fiascos in Nigeria, Angola, and elsewhere in Africa. The response by development, human rights, and environmental NGOs differed from earlier cases. Organizations from all three sectors were involved early, often in a coordinated way, sometimes producing joint papers, reports, statements, and strategies.

The project was to involve an unprecedented set of safeguards to ensure that oil revenues promoted broadly based development. It required government certification of how revenues were spent, it required a portion of the revenues be set aside for projects in areas impacted by the oil exploration and pipeline, and it required project-mandated national and international bodies to monitor the fulfillment of these conditions. But political instability, conflict, and both governments' weak human rights and governance records meant that NGOs were on the alert early, and environmental, development, and human rights advocates were ready and, to an unprecedented degree, united.

Catholic Relief Services (CRS) moved in 1998, during project planning, to work with the Cameroonian Center for the Environment and Development in advancing CRS's agenda of monitoring human rights and livelihood impacts of the pipeline project and arguing for just compensation of pipeline workers and of persons who were relocated or lost assets (trees, cropland) to make way for the pipeline. Also by September of 1998, eighty-six NGOs from twenty-eight countries had signed a letter to James Wolfensohn, president of the World Bank, citing human rights concerns and calling for the World Bank to halt preparations to finance the project (Horta 1998).

Mobilized by the Nigerian experience and equipped with special programs and projects that addressed corporate behavior and human rights/environment links, Amnesty International and Human Rights Watch did far more than simply report violations in their annual global human rights surveys. For Amnesty International, the vehicle for action was its "Just Earth!" program, which argued that in the context of civil war and ongoing humans rights violations, the loan to Chad was certain to produce further abuses (Amnesty International USA n.d.). Amnesty International's 1997 and 1998 reporting on massacres near the project site were widely cited in letters and reports by development and environmental NGOs (Amnesty International 1998; see Horta 1998). Amnesty International USA also made the pipeline a case in its corporate program beginning in 1999. Corporate responsibility was the key theme for Human Rights Watch. Its 1999 report on Nigeria, *The Price of Oil*, established corporate responsibility on the HRW agenda, and the Chad-Cameroon campaign figured prominently in the organization's "special issues and campaigns" on corporations and human rights (Human Rights Watch 1999).

The Chad-Cameroon campaign broke the pattern of earlier dam and pipeline advocacy, as development and human rights NGOs entered the debate immediately. In Narmada and most other prior cases, international environmental NGOs had led the advocacy effort, with development NGOs playing a minor role and international human rights NGOs joining when reports of civil and political rights violations began to circulate. But in Chad-Cameroon, Catholic Relief Services, which had worked in Cameroon since 1968 and had strong relationships with national Catholic institutions, entered the debate from the beginning and worked to strengthen local monitoring of the project. Oxfam America was also involved at least by September 2000. From the early stages of the campaign, the three sectors articulated a common message: poor countries such as Chad and Cameroon do deserve international assistance to profit from their untapped oil wealth, but only if effective safeguards can ensure that oil extraction itself respects detailed environmental safeguards and respects and compensates communities and that oil revenues will not be used to finance armed repression of the government's opponents (International Finance Corporation n.d.).

Interaction among international NGO participants across human rights–development–environment lines intensified dramatically. The activists make frequent references to each others' reports and demands in their correspondence with the World Bank and other authorities. Among the principal international NGO advocates involved, the Bank Information Center (BIC) and Catholic Relief Services adopted a joint strategy and produced joint publications as part of the monitoring process, taking advantage of CRS's strong contacts in the countries and BIC's experience with World Bank–financed projects. BIC, CRS, and the Environmental Defense Fund published a joint report in April 2004; CRS and BIC followed up in July; BIC and CRS in February 2005; BIC, Friends of the Earth, and Oxfam International in 2005.

The Chad-Cameroon pipeline may be nearly unique in its level of international human rights–development–environment NGO cooperation. But the pattern it represents is clear. By engaging themselves in the struggles over controversial large-scale infrastructure and major extractive industry projects that provoked local resistance, international NGOs in environment, development, and human rights became increasingly familiar and engaged with each other's methods and objectives. While full, joint participation in shared initiatives remained rare, the groundwork was being laid for further integration. A series of global conferences during the 1990s further reinforced this trend.

TOWARD SHARED AGENDAS AT THE GLOBAL CONFERENCES OF THE 1990s

The UN-sponsored global conferences during the 1990s became occasions for NGO lobbying of the official meetings, as well as for parallel, simultaneous NGO events. The meetings, especially on the environment, social policy, human rights, and women, were occasions for disagreement, negotiation, and building understanding among NGOs across North-South lines. Equally important, interactions occurred across the human rights–development frontier, and with women's movements and indigenous rights advocates playing pivotal, catalytic roles, the conferences deepened awareness of the possibilities for more cooperative and united action.

The global conferences have been followed closely by scholars interested in social policy issues and in the growing NGO engagement in global governance. The more specialized, issue-focused conferences on human habitat and on population and development have been the basis for important new monitoring efforts, but it is the broader conferences on the environment, human rights, women and development, and social development—where development and human rights advocates come together and engage in debates within the NGO community as well as with governmental participants—that are of greatest interest here.

Friedman, Hochstetler, and Clark (2005) document the growing links among NGO sectors at the environment, human rights, and women's conferences in 1992, 1993, and 1995. Their research, which unfortunately does not include the World Summit on Social Development (WSSD), demonstrates a pattern that is replicated in the social summit: women's organizations play a critical role in bridging the gap between human rights agendas and the social policy issues that are the focus of development NGOs.

At the 1993 World Conference on Human Rights in Vienna, women from around the world were at the forefront of mobilizations for the recognition that women's rights are human rights. While issues of violence against women were central to the debates at the Vienna meeting, poverty, lack of access to education, land, and resources were also debated as barriers to meeting women's fundamental rights. Women's groups' steadfast defense of the universality and indivisibility of human rights shored up those human rights positions at the rancorous conference (Dorsey 1996; Friedman, Hochstetler and Clark 2005) and paved the way for stronger linkages between human rights and development activists, for the reintegration of civil and political rights with ESC rights, and for understanding rights-based approaches to development.

At the WSSD in Copenhagen, the theme was further elaborated, as the language of "women in development" or "gender and development" intersected with the "women's rights as human rights" frame that had become a dominant element of women's advocates' approach. The Women's Caucus, in preparation for the WSSD, agreed on an agenda that advanced gender issues in social development by using both human rights and development concepts. The caucus agenda included improving gender analysis of the eradication of poverty, improving employment opportunities, and promoting social integration, and it called for a new paradigm in development that would revalue women's contributions to national economies and societies, redistribute resources, and strengthen the legal mechanisms that ensure women's human rights (Friedman 2003; Moghadam 2005).

Throughout the conferences, and particularly at Copenhagen, human rights and development organizations encountered and became familiar with alternative analytical frameworks and rhetorical approaches to key economic and social policy issues, including structural adjustment, labor market participation, and social and political participation.

Converging Agendas, New Organizations, Shared Initiatives, Methods, and Identities

A flood of new initiatives and newly founded organizations on the human rights–development frontier are the most visible manifestations of the convergence that accelerated in the 1990s. Less readily observable, but equally important, are the convergence of agendas and shifting methods and identities that occurred across the international NGO world. In this section we document these trends, then profile the alliances, campaigns, and hybrid organizations that form the most dynamic element of the human rights–development nexus.

COMMON AGENDAS

Working in local and global arenas during the 1980s and early 1990s, international human rights and development NGOs, along with environmental, women's, and indigenous people's organizations, pursued agendas that were sometimes closely related. During the debates over dam projects and oil pipelines and in discussions related to the UN global conferences, NGOs in the two sectors repeatedly found they were working in parallel on common priorities, sometimes using different language and even conceptual frames.

Development NGOs, for example, were promoting guidelines and practices to increase "popular participation" in projects funded by major donors, while human rights NGOs were insisting on the "right to participation" in decisions affecting people's lives and future choices. Development advocacy organizations placed emphasis on protecting "vulnerable populations" from the effects of infrastructure projects, from other threats related to conflict, natural disaster, or economic shocks, and from reductions in government services brought on by budgetary constraints. Human rights NGOs pursued similar objectives, invoking the principle of nondiscrimination. What development advocates referred to as fair compensation to people involuntarily resettled for major projects was addressed by human rights NGOs as remedies for human rights violations.

In short, while the degree of convergence during this period was modest, and the incidence of shared initiatives and joint planning infrequent, the growing awareness of common agendas was preparing the way for more substantial forms of collaboration in the years to come.

NEW ORGANIZATIONS, INITIATIVES, METHODS, AND IDENTITIES

These shared agendas were not the only product to emerge from advocacy experiences in the 1980s and early 1990s. Among organizations, at the individual level and across the sectors, these interactions spawned a generation of new NGOs and campaigns, new relationships, new and more flexible identities, and new skills and methods. By the mid-1990s, the result was a global collection of human rights, development, women's, and environmental NGOs that was more diverse, better networked, and more familiar with each others' agendas and methods.

New Organizations

The global conferences, particularly those on women and on social development, led to the creation of international NGOs that now play important roles in animating the human rights–development exchange. A striking list of new international NGOs emerged at the time of the preparation for and monitoring of the global conferences.

MADRE (founded in 1983), International Women's Health Coalition (1984), Women's Environment and Development Organization (1990), Women for Women International (1993), Social Watch (1995), and many others were founded during the period of the global conferences or played vital roles in coordinating NGO participation.

The Women's Environment and Development Organization (WEDO), for example, was founded in 1990 to promote "a healthy and peaceful planet, economic and social justice, and human rights for all." WEDO played a leading role in work on women's rights in development throughout the 1990s; it was launched with the World Women's Congress for a Healthy Planet, in preparation for the 1992 UNCED Conference, and played key roles in facilitating women's caucuses at Cairo and succeeding conferences. WEDO's explicit goal was to unite and strengthen the voice of women's organizations by articulating common themes and strategies throughout the UN global conferences. WEDO trained women's organizations, particularly NGOs based in the global South, on UN processes and on lobbying strategies needed to give prominence to women's policy priorities.

International Women's Health Coalition, founded in the United States in 1984, established its international identity while playing a central role in women's movement representation at Beijing and Cairo. Social Watch, an NGO network with an international secretariat at the Instituto Tercer Mundo (Third World Institute) in Montevideo, Uruguay, was chartered in 1995–96 to monitor commitments made at the Women's Conference and Social Summit. Social Watch has become an authoritative NGO voice whose monitoring agenda spans economic and social policy and human rights concerns.

Similarly, the international campaigns to influence large-scale, controversial development projects also spawned a set of new organizations, some of which became central players or important catalysts in later campaigns that brought human rights and development agendas, organizations, and strategies together more decisively. The Bank Information Center (BIC), created in Washington, D.C., in 1987, and the Bretton Woods Project, created in 1995 in London, both disseminate information and analysis about the multilateral development banks. BIC grew rapidly to serve activists and community organizations in the poor countries with access to information from the World Bank and logistical assistance in Washington. Bretton Woods Project, whose analysis and information services also extend to NGOs globally, was created in London by the Development and Environment Group, a caucus of British NGOs.

International Rivers Network, active in the United States since 1985, began international work in 1989. "Linking human rights and environmental protection," International Rivers Network (now known as International Rivers) became the premier activist organization on dam and river issues, linking to European and Southeast Asian Rivers Networks and to dozens of NGOs worldwide.

A longer list of international NGOs created between 1980 and the mid-1990s, in table 4.1, includes organizations that have in common their origins in the local battles or global conferences. Their global networking, their embrace of popular participation, transparency, "defending the defenders" strategies, and nondiscrimination, together with their willingness to cross over the human rights, development, and environmental NGO lines by adopting new agendas, methods, and strategies, make them essential to the growth of new rights advocacy movements.

New Initiatives, Skills, and Methods

Interaction in global meetings and local campaigns introduced NGOs in each sector to new methods and skills and sometimes produced new cross-sector initiatives. Defending the Defenders, a joint campaign of Amnesty International USA and the Sierra Club launched in 1998, focused on defending the human rights of environmental advocates, symbolized during the 1990s by the murder of Chico Mendes of the Brazilian rubber tappers' union, and used Amnesty International–style urgent actions to respond to the plights of individual environmental activists.

Amnesty International and Human Rights Watch both initiated projects on corporate responsibility and human rights, beginning the

Table 4.1 Newly Created NGOs

NAME, COUNTRY	DATE	MISSION
Bretton Woods Project, UK	1995	"Scrutinise and monitor" World Bank and IMF through research, reports, briefings, bimonthly alerts
Rainforest Action Network	1985	"Campaigns for the forests, their inhabitants and the natural systems that sustain life, by transforming the global marketplace"
Bank Information Center, USA	1987	"Protection of rights, participation, transparency, and public accountability" at the multilateral development banks
International Rivers Network, USA	1985	Reporting, advocacy, and capacity building work on the environmental and human rights impact
PROBE, Canada	1980	"Expose the environmental, social and economic effects of Canada's aid abroad"
Global Exchange, USA	1988	"Human rights organization promoting . . . economic, social and environmental justice"
Article 19, UK	1987	Freedom of expression and freedom of information; national and international rules and legislation, grounded in UDHR Article 19
Center for International Environmental Law	1989	HR/environment program (1998): "identify and develop connections" . . . "integrate the theoretical and advocacy approaches of the two movements"
Global Response	1990	Environmental activism, response to indigenous communities' requests
WEED, Germany	1990	Link ecological and antipoverty work
Global Witness London	1993	Field investigations and reporting in situations of conflict, corruption and human rights abuse
Halifax Initiative, Canada	1994	"Transform the international financial system . . . to achieve poverty eradication, environmental sustainability and the full realization of HRs"
EarthRights International, USA	1996	Community organizing and education, litigation, advocacy, training for activists
Project Underground	1996	"Environmental, human rights and indigenous rights . . . campaigns against abusive extractive resource activity"
Cornerhouse, UK	1997	"Support democratic and community movements for environmental and social justice"
Mekong Watch, Japan	1993	Respect of views of affected communities, learning from past projects
European Rivers Network	1994	To link and coordinate groups active on river basin issues, especially across human rights environment, culture, education fields

shift from a nearly complete focus on states as human rights guarantors and violators. Amnesty International's Corporate Action Network features urgent action alerts, advocacy in support of the UN Norms for Transnational Business and Human Rights, leadership of the International Right to Know Campaign, and a corporate shareholder lobbying initiative. Human Rights Watch's earliest research reports on corporate conduct included studies in 1996 on bonded labor in India, sex discrimination and labor standards in Mexican *maquiladoras*, labor rights and the North American Free Trade Agreement (NAFTA), and "contemporary forms of slavery" in Pakistan.

Human rights–specific methods and skills, especially investigation and documentation of rights violations, entered into the repertoire of environment and development NGOs. The integrated medical relief and reporting work of Médecins Sans Frontières (MSF), the planned and coordinated monitoring that Catholic Relief Services has carried out in Chad and Cameroon, and the access to information and anticorruption work of ActionAid in India all indicate a new openness to and familiarity with human rights methods.

Supporting local partner organizations in asserting, monitoring, and protecting human rights is not a new practice for NGOs such as ActionAid and the Oxfams, which rely heavily on grant making to local partners. But other international development NGOs broadened their human rights–related organizational support capacities and skills, including CARE in parts of Africa, and Catholic Relief Services in African countries following the Rwandan genocide (Goulet 2002).

Development NGOs' participants in the WSSD renewed or deepened their knowledge of human rights approaches to social and economic policy, especially the application of economic and social rights. Social Watch's monitoring of the WSSD implementation, for example, adopts the human rights language and methodology of "mobilizing shame" (Roque 2003), and the network has become actively involved in promoting ESC rights approaches, especially in Latin America.

Even as organizational identities became more fluid with the introduction of new skills and initiatives, professional and political identities became more multifaceted as individuals strengthened skills and relationships across sector lines. Some of this movement occurs in areas such as refugee policy, where humanitarian assistance and advocacy for refugee rights have overlapped for some time, and in work on HIV/AIDS and issue areas such as debt.

All these changes—new initiatives, organizations, coalitions, and identities—brought some within the human rights and development fields to a state of readiness for more decisive breaching of the old divides between the fields. In the sections that follow, the interaction deepens, first through shared advocacy on international issue campaigns, then through deeper, more integrated new rights campaigns on water and HIV/AIDS.

NEW ALLIANCES FOR COLLABORATIVE ISSUE CAMPAIGNS

The most visible manifestation of this deepening interaction has been a set of campaigns engaging NGOs from the human rights, environment, and development sectors in work on shared agendas. Worldwide, networks and alliances coordinating issue-specific campaigns sprouted at an accelerating rate throughout the 1990s, or rose from relative obscurity to become household names during the decade. Many of these are also settings in which human rights and development practitioners cooperate and collaborate, deepening their knowledge of each sector's methods and building relationships and trust without necessarily committing to joint strategies or taking steps that change the core activities of the member NGOs.

The Clean Diamonds Campaign, efforts to force information disclosure by international corporations, debt relief, and the child soldiers campaigns have in common their diverse coalitions, loose networking organizational form, and their use of human rights language. The diamonds and information campaigns target the behavior of international corporations, broadening and deepening the corporate social responsibility movement (Newell 2000).

The Clean Diamonds Campaign features cooperation among governments and NGOs, including mainstream development aid providers such as World Vision and human rights NGOs such as

Amnesty International (Smillie and Gberie 2001). The campaign attempts to regulate the diamond industry's purchase and sale of diamonds controlled by military factions in war-torn Sierra Leone, Liberia, and elsewhere. After several years of NGO pressure, the creation of the Kimberley Process in 2003 to track diamonds from mine to jewelers' display cases, and extended debate over the adequacy and reliability of the process, debate remains lively in 2006 (Maung 2006), with Amnesty International, Oxfam, and Global Witness playing leading roles.

The International Campaign for a Right to Know (IRTK) involves development, environment, and human rights NGOs calling for expanded disclosure requirements for U.S.-based multinationals. After the 1984 Union Carbide Bhopal disaster, the U.S. Congress enacted legislation in 1986 requiring American companies operating in the United States to release information regarding operations involving toxic chemicals. The IRTK campaign proposes to extend these requirements to the foreign operations of U.S.-based companies, requiring them to disclose security arrangements, human rights practices, labor standards, environmental policies, and toxic releases.

Established in 2003 by a founding group including the AFL-CIO, Amnesty International USA, EarthRights International, Friends of the Earth, Global Exchange, Oxfam America, and Sierra Club, the campaign is backed by case studies of oil spills, abuses by private security forces, illegal land appropriations, and child labor (International Right to Know Campaign 2003). Launched in the United States, IRTK now includes two hundred members and is tied to initiatives in other countries.

The Publish What You Pay Campaign calls on international corporations in extractive industries (mining, oil, and gas) to disclose their payments to all governments. Launched in 2002 by Global Witness, the English/Welsh Catholic agency CAFOD, Oxfam, Save the Children UK, Transparency International UK, and Soros, the list of 280 NGO endorsers reflects the strong development emphasis of the founders, but it also includes specialized corporate accountability NGOs, three national sections of Amnesty International, Human

Rights Watch, and other human rights NGOs (Publish What You Pay 2005). Disclosing corporate payments to governments is intended to "help citizens of resource-rich developing countries hold their governments accountable for the management of these revenues" (Publish What You Pay n.d.). The campaign is linked to NGO advocacy for transparency at the multilateral development banks (Nelson 2003) and for the rights to freedom of expression and information by NGOs such as London-based Article 19.

The international campaign against the use of child soldiers in state and nonstate militaries is coordinated by the London-based Coalition to Stop the Use of Child Soldiers, formed in 1998. Its steering group includes human rights, development, and peace activists, including Amnesty International, Human Rights Watch, International Federation Terre des Hommes, International Save the Children Alliance, Jesuit Refugee Service, the Quaker United Nations Office–Geneva, and World Vision International. The Coalition works with UNICEF and the International Committee of the Red Cross and with national networks in twenty-seven countries and the European Union. The campaign, grounded in the human rights world, has attracted development NGOs. National secretariats include offices of World Vision (Canada), UNICEF (Netherlands and Belgium), Save the Children (Uganda), the International Rescue Committee (Uganda), and Terre des Hommes (Germany).

Debt Relief advocates, led by Oxfam GB, the Washington-based Center of Concern, and several faith-based NGOs, have worked since the early 1980s to convince major creditor governments to soften the terms of repayment and make other reforms to lighten the burden of servicing debt owed to international creditors (Donnelly 2002). After minor changes to repayment terms during the 1980s and early 1990s, NGOs in Africa, Europe, and the United States launched the Jubilee campaign in a more sustained effort to force the World Bank and the International Monetary Fund (IMF) to write off significant debt owed to them by the lowest income, most deeply indebted countries. Jubilee-2000 and its successors have been largely led by faith-based NGOs, specialized issue-based organizations, and several principal development NGOs, especially Oxfam and the European Network on Debt and Development (EURODAD).

Despite initiatives such as that of Africa Action, international human rights NGOs have been minor players, addressing debt issues only in passing. But a special rapporteur's report to the UN Human Rights Committee and a number of social justice and development organizations have embraced human rights approaches to the debt crisis, arguing against the legitimacy of debt incurred by dictatorial regimes, drawing on the concept of the "right to development," or arguing that ESC rights have been compromised by the costs of debt servicing. The New Economics Foundation proposes an approach to identifying sustainable levels of debt, based on human rights standards and logic rather than primarily on macroeconomic calculations (Mandel 2006).

A long list of initiatives involve participants from the two sectors in various styles and levels of collaboration, including the International Campaign to Ban Land Mines, Pesticide Action Network (PANNA 2005), networks promoting labor rights and opposing female genital cutting, child soldiers, and sweatshops.

These initiatives meet the minimal standard of involving development and human rights NGOs actively in the network, and they represent a new level of intersectoral cooperation and collaboration. In earlier cases of interaction in the 1980s and 1990s, NGOs from the two sectors stopped short of forming united movements or adopting common strategies. Here, collaboration involves joint commitments, memberships, affiliations, copublishing, and, in some cases, joint decision-making bodies. We will discuss the significance of this collaboration and its relation to the problematic issues that have been raised with respect to NGO issue networks in the chapter's final section.

CONVERGENT NEW RIGHTS ALLIANCES FEATURING SHARED METHODS AND JOINT INITIATIVES

New rights campaigns have also taken up economic and social human rights standards and used them as leverage over social policy issues.[1]

In two current cases, NGOs and social movements are advocating for broader access to essential medicines, particularly for those affected by HIV/AIDS, and for protection of the right of access to drinking water in the context of rapid privatization of water utilities. The cooperation and joint efforts among NGOs, consumer organizations, and other movements are evidence of a new level of integration in which methods, language, strategies, and actions are consistently informed by the human rights–development interaction.

These convergent new rights campaigns are distinguished from the coalition work discussed above by the level of integration of human rights strategies and by their emergence from initiatives in the global South. South Africa's Treatment Action Campaign, Kenya's Greenbelt Movement, various national coalitions for the right to water, and Brazil's Landless Rural Workers' Movement are examples of movements of some of their societies' most marginalized people making radical, rights-based claims on their governments and winning widespread international support.

HIV/AIDS

Advocacy for the right of access to HIV/AIDS treatment exemplifies the characteristics of some of the new rights advocacy. It has involved close cooperation with governments (Brazil, South Africa, India), strong North-South links between activist movements, and appeals to ESC rights standards as a counterweight to corporate power and to liberal trade rules and economic policies.

Much international HIV/AIDS advocacy explicitly argues that access to care for HIV-infected patients is an essential component of the internationally recognized human right to the "highest attainable standard" of health (International Covenant on Economic, Social and Cultural Rights Article 11; 't Hoen 2000; Health GAP 2006; Oxfam International 2002b). According to Ziti (quoted in Berkman 2001), human rights standards serve HIV/AIDS policy and practice as "a body of international law, a set of norms for governmental behavior, and as a strategic tool for social change." The AIDS advocacy movement is vast and diverse, and our interest is limited to the role of human rights principles and methods and their impact on the pattern of government-NGO contestation and cooperation.

Advocates for a strong human rights–based response have emphasized four themes since the mid-1990s: the demand for access to medicines, including the effort to overcome WTO trade rules and patent restrictions on their generic manufacture (Oxfam International 2001, 2002a); the protection of people with HIV/AIDS from discriminatory treatment; the call for funding for the United Nations' Global Fund to Fight HIV/AIDS, Malaria and Tuberculosis; and the campaign to influence the behavior of pharmaceutical companies. Médecins Sans Frontières (MSF) and the South African Treatment Action Campaign (TAC), traditional human rights organizations such as Physicians for Human Rights, Global Treatment Access Network, and the Health Global Access Project (GAP), and AIDS activist organizations in the United States and Europe have all provided leadership in the international human rights–based movement on HIV/AIDS.

Advocating for expanded aid by wealthy-country governments is not a new theme for development NGOs, which have called for more generous official aid allocations for decades. Human rights NGOs joined in the effort to encourage full funding of the UN's Global Fund, invoking the human rights obligation of wealthy-country governments to contribute and seeking to shift the framing of the issue from aid as charity to aid as fulfillment of a fundamental right (Amnesty International 2006).

The civil and political rights of HIV/AIDS patients are the principal focus of Human Rights Watch's AIDS program. Applying its research and documentation methods, HRW demonstrates that discrimination and stigmatization, and sometimes systematic violations of the civil and political rights of people living with HIV/AIDS, contribute to their reluctance to seek testing and treatment. Under these circumstances, improved protection of rights against discrimination is a step to improve testing and treatment.[2]

But arguably the most dramatic and significant implications of human rights for AIDS advocacy have been manifested in advocates' work on two related issues: governments' policies for the provision of treatment to HIV patients, and the international collision of property rights and human rights in debates over trade rules related to intellectual property rights (TRIPs). In promoting access to treatment, for example, NGO advocates often ally themselves with poor-country governments in an effort to limit, change, or circumvent the rules or authority of international organizations.

Advocates in South Africa and in international arenas invoked international human rights and constitutional rights derived from them in four ways: local and national education and mobilization, national litigation, international lobbying to stop suits and legal challenges by pharmaceutical companies and the U.S. government, and formal arguments in the WTO to soften patent and TRIPs rules regarding generics.

Despite their criticism of the government, domestic and international advocates continued to cooperate with the state throughout the 1990s. Initiatives by the governments of South Africa and Brazil to produce generic versions of patented antiretroviral drugs led to threats of formal action against them—a suit by the U.S. government against South Africa and action under WTO rules against Brazil. NGO activists gave unusually strong and direct support to government initiatives, as the following profile of the work of MSF with the governments of South Africa and Brazil demonstrates.

MSF's goals are "to support health ministries that are fighting to increase access to essential drugs" and to "support the implementation of existing trade rules . . . designed to protect" access to these medicines by informing and advising governments on their options (Médecins Sans Frontières 2002b). During clinical trials of antiretroviral drugs in South Africa in 2002, MSF negotiated with the South African and Brazilian governments to purchase and export to South Africa generic versions at roughly half the cost of those available from multinational pharmaceutical companies (Médecins Sans Frontières 2002a).

South African activists from the Treatment Action Campaign (TAC) participated in the transactions and in MSF's clinical trials, and they sided with the South African government in the lawsuit against it by the Pharmaceutical Manufacturers Association (PMA). This cooperative strategy was pursued even as TAC continued the advocacy that eventually led to the cabinet's November 2003 commitment to making antiretroviral treatment available in every government health facility to people with HIV. PMA abandoned the legal action soon after TAC entered the case.

This high-profile national policy debate was intertwined with the global debate over the relationship between patent and property rights in the WTO's TRIPs standards and the human right to health. AIDS activists appeared to win a partial victory in 2001 when the Doha Ministerial Meeting reaffirmed that governments' right to act in a public health emergency superseded intellectual property rights. The Meeting's Declaration on TRIPs and Public Health created a temporary (fifteen-year) exception to assure that TRIPs did not prevent countries from taking steps to promote public health.

This ruling opened a further debate over the mechanisms by which poor-country governments can act. For countries without capacity to produce generic antiretrovirals, a low-cost and efficient mechanism for trade in these generic drugs is essential, and a temporary mechanism was created in August 2003 and adopted in Hong Kong in December 2005. Critics argue that the mechanism's case-by-case approval approach, designed to ensure that no generic drugs find their way into industrial country markets, is "burdensome and unworkable" (Joint Statement by NGOs 2005).

HIV/AIDS advocates have also directly engaged the pharmaceutical companies that hold patents on the drugs used to treat HIV infection. Oxfam mounted sustained advocacy focused on the pharmaceutical giants Pfizer and GlaxoSmithKline, pursuing both public and private efforts to persuade the companies to adjust the prices in poor countries. Oxfam's (2001, 2002c) reports on the pharmaceutical industry—one subtitled "Patient Rights before Patent Rights"—are directed to the firms themselves and to key government bodies such as the UK Parliament in an effort to shape public and governmental perceptions of the industry and to soften the industry's position on trade and patent rules.

Right to Water

Human rights standards are being invoked to guarantee universal access to adequate supplies of safe drinking water. The human right to water is recognized in the Convention on the Elimination of All Forms of Discrimination Against Women (CEDAW, Article 14(2)(h)) and in the Convention on the Rights of the Child (Article 24) and was reinforced in November 2002 when the UN Committee on Economic, Social and Cultural Rights issued an explanatory General Comment 15, making explicit the ICESCR's guarantee of a right to water (Committee on Economic, Social and Cultural Rights 2002).

But water rights advocates confront a powerful set of norms emphasizing market mechanisms and the benefits of economic openness and reduced government roles in the economy, norms that Goldman (2005) shows have been effectively promoted for water services by the World Bank and global water corporations. Market-led development, even with the now conventional modifiers that recognize the need for "broad-based" growth, investment in human capital, and good governance, does not coexist comfortably with a framework for development built on guarantees of universal rights. Asserting universal rights to water is in part a means of gaining leverage against market-based development policy.

At least fourteen countries in sub-Saharan Africa, and numerous countries and municipalities elsewhere, are implementing or considering dramatic changes to water supply systems (Hall, Bayliss, and Lobina 2002; Grusky 2001). Encouraged by the World Bank and/or the IMF (Hall, Bayliss, and Lobina 2002), the new policies involve a shift from state-managed water provision to provision by the private sector, usually international contractors, with fees paid by end users. The Water Observatory's document archive provides a thorough record of social movement and NGO advocacy, making it possible to trace the references to economic and social rights over the course of national debates (Water Observatory n.d).

There is often a good case for reworking these water systems. Many state-managed systems, while providing drinking water at little or no cost to some citizen-clients, are plagued by high administrative costs, financial losses, leakage, and inadequate coverage, especially of poor "customers" (Globalization Challenge Initiative 2001).

But in virtually every municipality and country where privatization has been proposed, resistance has been vigorous and has made reference to international human rights (Ghana National Coalition 2001) or to national constitutional or statutory guarantees (SAMWU 2002). Anticipated increases in water fees are the universal factor motivating opposition, usually accompanied by other grievances. In Ghana and Bolivia, governments agreed in 1999 to new municipal water delivery systems managed by private contractors and financed in part by user fees. Local consumer movements, national and international NGOs have all either resisted privatization or advanced proposals to modify contract arrangements.

The Coalition against Privatisation of Water in Ghana (the "National Coalition") objected to the government's "fast track" implementation of privatization, the lack of transparency in preparing contracts, and the perceived favoring of multinational corporations (Ghana National Coalition 2001). The Ghanaian campaign gained international support from NGOs already critical of the World Bank's privatization agenda (Grusky 2001; International Water Working Group 2002). Ghanaian advocates also reached out to international opponents of privatization through speaking tours and by sponsoring an international fact-finding tour to Ghana (Amenga-Etego and Grusky 2005, 285).

In India, human rights arguments are prominent in legal and political challenges to the National Water Policy of 2002, which provided for private ownership and management of water systems (Pant 2003). Human rights are similarly invoked in opposition to corporate use of water resources, especially by soft-drink bottlers (Vidal 2003).

In South Africa, the movement for the human right to water was galvanized by private water providers' use of prepaid water meters on village and neighborhood pumps. These meters, which allow water to flow only to those who have paid in advance, sharpened the perception that privatized water systems will involve systematic violations of poor citizens' rights (Anti-Privatisation Forum 2003; Marvin, Laurie, and Napier 2001).

Through the 1990s, international support for these movements took three primary forms: small solidarity networks with links to a country or city; antiprivatization advocates working on privatization issues at the World Bank and the IMF; and anticorporate globalization activists such as the Canadian Blue Planet Network. All used the language of rights, without specific reference to international agreements, and mobilized individuals and organizations around the principle that "water is a fundamental, inalienable individual and collective right," and that "it is up to society as a whole to guarantee the right of access . . . without discrimination" (Global Committee for the Water Contract 1998). They urged governments to pledge "not to privatize, trade, export water, and to exempt water from trade and investment agreements" (Blue Planet Project 2001).

The pace and intensity of international water advocacy grew rapidly after General Comment 15 on the right to water was released in 2002. Three international NGOs exemplify the dominant role of the human rights frame. The New York–based Center for Economic and Social Rights (CESR) (2001) advocates a human rights–based approach, refers to human rights agreements and affirmations of the right to water in national constitutions, and ties the human right to water to the World Health Organization's standards of access to twenty to forty liters of water daily, "within a reasonable distance from the household."

The International Water Working Group (IWWG), headquartered at Washington, D.C.–based Public Citizen, focuses its advocacy work on the IMF, the World Bank, and the WTO's General Agreement on Trade in Services (GATS). In 2003, IWWG began making specific reference to water as a human right, and it has now assembled a thorough analysis of the use of prepaid water meters (International Water Working Group 2004). Other South African and international advocacy organizations take similar positions (Concannon and Griffiths 2001). The UK-based NGO WaterAid adopted a "human rights approach" in 2003, with implications for its water-related project assistance (Water Aid n.d.) and for its advocacy work, which includes a critique of "private sector participation" in water system reforms (Water Aid 2003).

A flood of new reports, position papers, and advocacy initiatives has appeared since 2002, by the German NGOs Brot für die Welt and WEED (Hoering and Schneider 2004); Jubilee South (Laifungbam 2003); Amnesty International (2003); and COHRE (2004c). Reports by WHO (2003) and WHO, COHRE, and the American Association for the Advancement of Science (2004) also frame water as a human rights issue. As Conca (2005) finds in his study of the international governance of water, human rights became the dominant frame used by privatization opponents.

Although the record of national litigation is growing (COHRE 2004c), the use of international human rights law on water is not well developed (Weiss, de Chazournes, and Bernasconi-Osterwalder 2005). The appeal to human rights standards on water has been primarily political, not legal. It adds rhetorical power and moral authority to advocates' case for universal access, and it offers an alternative framework to the dominant emphasis on economic efficiency of market mechanisms. Water advocates have often succeeded in blocking or modifying privatization agreements, perhaps most famously in Cochabamba, Bolivia (Sustainability Review 2006). To date there is less evidence that they have succeeded in pressing governments for more satisfactory public service where privatization has failed, although there are initiatives under way to study public alternatives to privatization.

CAMPAIGNS AND INTRA-NGO POLITICS

What light do these campaigns and alliances shed on current scholarly discussions regarding the power relations inherent in North-South NGO "partnerships"? As noted in chapter 1, North American and European NGOs do enjoy clear advantages of resources and access to powerful governments and international institutions, and it is hard to deny that funding arrangements in the development sector place international NGOs in a position of control. Clifford Bob

(2005) argues that the same is true of environmental and human rights advocates. Bob's research, which shows that international NGOs can serve as gatekeepers that control access by communities or movements to the international media and international human rights mechanisms, captures an important dimension of power relationships among NGOs.

But the alliances and new rights campaigns discussed here suggest two additional important considerations. First, many such international campaigns are not focused on single, localized grievances but involve systemic international issues and proposals. Proposals by advocates of the international right to know, Publish What You Pay, debt relief, TRIPs rules, child soldiers, and many others are systemic proposals that may be rooted in a history of specific, localized incidents but do not directly involve any "gatekeeper" role by international NGOs.

Second, the fact that international NGOs can often be strategic and selective in choosing among deserving human rights claims to contest at the international level has a corollary. There are social movements whose dynamism makes it essential for international NGOs to be associated with them, and whose strategies help to lead international NGOs toward human rights–based approaches to major social policy issues. Movements such as the Treatment Action Campaign, Greenbelt Movement in Kenya, and the Landless Rural Workers Movement in Brazil (MST) have won international support for rights-based demands made both in national and international contexts.

The South African Treatment Action Campaign (TAC), for example, as Friedman and Mottiar (2005) show, has made the human right to health and to freedom from discrimination central to its highly effective campaign for a commitment from the South African government to provide treatment to all HIV patients. The moral authority of TAC's rights-based campaign has been successful in driving domestic AIDS policy, despite the South African government's reluctance. The moral case TAC has constructed, anchored in internationally recognized human rights and their expression in the South African constitution, constitutes a common moral discourse and a source of power for a social movement such as TAC.

TAC's approach has attracted support from official donors, foundations, and international NGOs including, in 2005 alone, two national Oxfam affiliates, Brot für die Welt, MSF, the Dutch development NGO Hivos, and the American Jewish World Service; foundations including Ford, Open Society Institute, Atlantic Philanthropies, and the Henry J. Kaiser Family Foundation; and several national aid agencies and embassies (Treatment Action Campaign 2005).

Creating Organizational Hybrids

A small number of organizations combine within them characteristics of both development and human rights NGOs. These NGOs carry out activities typical of both types, participate in networks and alliances of both human rights and development organizations, and use methods drawn from both fields. These NGOs include, for example, the International Women's Health Coalition, which practices a human rights–based approach to advocacy and programming for women's access to health services; EarthRights International, established during campaigns against Unocal corporate projects in Burma; and Dignity International, the Netherlands-based NGO that works with other NGOs to encourage rights-based development approaches.

Other international NGOs, such as the British Rights and Humanity and the European Terre des Hommes, also integrate human rights work and community development, but we limit ourselves to cases that thoroughly integrate methods and characteristics of the sectors. Each of these three is significant in itself, but what makes them worthy of attention is their power to shape other organizations around them. Each of these organizations is attracting a cluster of colleague and partner organizations whose framework and methodology are shaped by the hybrid's approach.

WHAT CONSTITUTES A HYBRID NGO?

The defining characteristics of "hybrid" organizations is the uniting of several core organizational features from fields that are usually divided: the NGO's mission, structure, funding sources, core working methodology, key association with others, staffing skills, and professions. Hybrid organizations integrate the sectors systematically, crossing sector lines in several of these features. In identifying and analyzing the hybrid NGOs discussed here, we have used these criteria:

- Founding and leadership involve founders or executive officers crossing sector lines, or individuals from more than one sector.

- Mission is stated in terms that embrace objectives of more than one sector.

- Funding does not draw exclusively on traditional sources for either sector, but involves official aid donors and foundations traditionally associated with each.

- Methodology brings together methods that dominate in the sectors: material aid, policy advocacy, capacity building, human rights reporting, education, litigation.

- Human rights and development functions are integrated, not strictly segmented. Human rights education or documentation is integrated with other kinds of program work, and the crossover is not limited to a single project or campaign.

- Staffing includes staff members with skills and backgrounds representing both sectors.

- Networks and Partnerships: The NGO is linked to a diverse set of partner and colleague agencies that cross sector boundaries.

Several organizations integrate the sectors in these ways, and most are relatively new. The picture that emerges from the brief, selective organizational profiles that follow is of a set of influential NGOs that present models for integrating human rights and development work. These models are being emulated by partner and counterpart organizations and promoted by a handful of influential funders.

International Women's Health Coalition

Adrienne Germaine and Joan Dunlop founded the International Women's Health Coalition (IWHC) in 1984. Germaine jokingly gives credit to then U.S. president Ronald Reagan, whose "global gag rule" denied U.S. funds to NGOs that support safe, legal abortions for poor women throughout the world, and was the impetus to IWHC's founding. From its beginning as a human rights and women's rights advocacy organization, it expanded its international network and its methodology to include close cooperation with local women's organizations in work that bridges the service delivery–human rights advocacy distinction.

Germaine's background in development work as program officer in South Asia for the Ford Foundation and Dunlop's history as an activist for women's reproductive rights brought together the development and human rights fields in IWHC's directorate. They also united development and human rights methodologies in a two-part strategy: build the social and political power of colleague agencies in the poor countries while working with them to deliver health services and education; and advocate in the international arena to reframe women's reproductive health from a "population" issue to a women's human rights issue.

Human rights education is an important component of IWHC's work with colleague agencies. IWHC supports women's organizations and health NGOs in promoting programmatic and policy solutions to the systematic denial of women's reproductive and sexual rights, adolescent's rights, and other health-related rights. The issue briefs on six key issues posted on the website feature services, policy priorities, and a summary of relevant standards in human rights agreements, capturing the blend of methods IWHC employs (see, e.g., International Women's Health Coalition n.d.).

Human rights education and advocacy are integrated with other forms of education and services, as in the IWHC-supported Girl's Power Initiative in Nigeria, which works with girls aged ten to eighteen to promote understanding of girls' (and women's) sexual and reproductive rights and to encourage critical analysis by male and female adolescents of prevailing social and cultural values and practices (International Women's Health Coalition 2002).

IWHC also serves as the secretariat for Health, Empowerment, Rights and Accountability (HERA), the group of twenty-four women's and human rights activists who helped to define the core of the agreements reached in Cairo and Beijing. Its members represent twenty-four organizations from eighteen countries, and although HERA does not list its affiliates, they include prominent advocates from Suriname, the United Kingdom, Mexico, and South Africa (HERA 1999). HERA's mission is to "advocate, and help design and implement strategies to guarantee sexual and reproductive rights and health, within a broader context of human rights and sustainable development" (HERA n.d.)

EarthRights International

EarthRights International (ERI) is the most self-conscious and deliberate of these hybrid NGOs in integrating methods and cultures. Founded in 1995 by veterans of the human rights and environmental campaigns over Unocal petroleum extraction and pipelines in Burma, ERI is directed by Ka Hsaw Wa, a human rights activist in Burma since 1988. Its U.S. and Southeast Asia offices are staffed by human rights investigators, educators and trainers, lawyers in human rights, environmental law, and dispute resolution, and specialists in fundraising, outreach, and administration.

The concept of earth rights is central to understanding ERI's mission and strategy. Earth rights are human rights with implications for the earth, including "the right to a healthy environment, the right to speak out and act to protect the environment, and the right to participate in development decisions." Earth rights, then, are human rights with respect to the environment, the rights of those individuals whose livelihoods and other rights are most directly and immediately tied to the ecosystem in which they live.

ERI is funded by grants from larger development NGOs (Oxfam America and Oxfam Hong Kong, American Jewish World Service, and others), by grants from foundations and NGOs in the human rights sector (Goldman Foundation, Rights and Democracy), as well as by major foundations including Ford, the Open Society Institute, and the Flora Family Foundation. It has loose ties, then, to the world of development aid donors through grant-making NGOs that are themselves not strongly tied to official donors.

ERI projects "promote and protect earth rights in different ways: by using the US or international legal system as a tool for change; by training and educating affected peoples so they become their own best advocates; by documenting, writing about, and publicizing abuses; by engaging international institutions . . . [and] by strengthening networks and coalitions" (EarthRights International n.d.).

In addition to advocacy and organizing work in Burma (the Burma Project), ERI has four broad projects: an EarthRights School, training environmental human rights activists in Southeast Asia; a women's project; an energy project focused on pipeline projects in the region; and a consumer advocacy projects called "USA Lead," which tries to influence U.S. consumer and investment practices to promote change in Burma. The ERI methodology summarizes its integrated methods:

> **Document human rights and environmental abuses,** and expose and publicize them; **organize and mobilize** the human rights and environmental activist communities around earth rights issues; **litigate** in U.S. courts on behalf of people around the world whose earth rights have been violated . . . **teach** people about their earth rights and remedies, especially people living under repressive regimes, by training villagers and refugee women and through the EarthRights Schools for activists . . . and **advocate** for those who have been harmed and fight for better earth rights protections at every level. (EarthRights International n.d.)

Much of ERI's "project" work consists of thematic advocacy and education projects. A close look at the project on mining and women illustrates the integration of human rights, environmental, and human development concerns. The ERI paper on mining and women is a subtle analysis of the different economic impacts of mining—through labor, investment, and other factors—on men and women. Family-owned mines and small operations have different implications for earth rights than do larger, foreign-owned mines, and ERI's analysis takes into account incomes, resource contamination, labor, and social and health impacts in developing a set of strategies for its work in the sector.

This kind of analysis is exemplary, and it is typical of ERI's practice of integrating socioeconomic analysis, at the community and larger levels, with human rights investigation and documentation. Human rights standards in this approach are legal tools at the international level and analytic and political tools at the local level, employed to produce analysis and strategy that informs the education of human rights activists, the design of advocacy programs, and the appeals to the U.S. media and consumers.

Dignity International

Dignity International, founded in the Netherlands in 1999 as a project of the North-South Centre of the Council of Europe, became an independent NGO in 2002. It promotes human rights–based strategies for social development by sponsoring training and networking opportunities regionally and globally, by helping to equip (mainly local and national) development NGOs with rights-based approaches and tools, and by sponsoring and supporting local projects. While its staff is primarily trained and experienced in human rights, it works with local, national, and community-based organizations of all kinds to educate, support, and build capacity for human rights–driven solutions to problems of social injustice. It supports, for example, human rights education programs in Portugal; housing rights activism in Mumbai, India; "people-led advocacy" efforts in sites such as slum settlements in Nairobi, Kenya; and "Learning and Linkages" programs on the application of human rights in local development in Tanzania (2006), Ecuador (2005), and Uruguay (2005). Its board members, funders, and organizational partnerships all reflect its ties to both the human rights and social development sectors.

Blurring the Sector Lines

Other international NGOs combine some features of human rights and development work. Global Witness, for example, uses investigative techniques to make the case for campaigns against governmental and corporate malfeasance in countries plagued by conflict or corruption. Its agenda has much in common with development and environmental advocacy groups—diamonds in West Africa, timber extraction in Cambodia, arms trafficking in Ukraine, oil in Angola—but its methods are a sometimes volatile mix of human rights investigation and journalistic reporting.

Médecins Sans Frontières (MSF), the international medical relief NGO whose practice of bearing witness to human rights conditions is discussed in chapter 3, took a further step toward the camp of human rights–development integrators in 1999 with its human rights–driven Campaign for Access to Essential Medicines. After decades of treating patients whose diseases are neglected by the market and by public health policy, MSF launched the campaign in 1999 to increase affordable access to the 206 drugs designated essential by the World Health Organization (MSF 2004).

The campaign's methods exemplify MSF's explicit and implicit integration of human rights and humanitarian concerns. It targets national governments, the pharmaceutical industry, and international organizations, encouraging expanded production, reduced prices, accelerated research and development, and trade rules that maximize access at affordable prices (Pécoul et al. 1999). The campaign also defends and promotes the WHO's role in international trade negotiations, encourages and defends national strategies now allowed under the WTO's TRIPs, and presses for generous funding of the Global Fund to Fight AIDS, Tuberculosis and Malaria.

Rights and Humanity aims to spread human rights–based principles through the daily practice of professions and through policy advocacy and programmatic work. The "international movement for the promotion and realization of human rights and responsibilities" is led by longtime human rights activist Julia Häusermann and engages in consultancies with national and UN donor agencies on the implementation of a rights-based approach to development.

Terre des Hommes and some of the members of the Save the Children Federation (in Sweden and the UK) integrate material assistance and human rights advocacy on issues involving children's rights.

WaterAid, the London-based development organization focused on water and sanitation issues, joined with the Freshwater Action Network in 2003 to create Right to Water, a web-based networking and advocacy tool that aims to promote understanding and implementation of water as a human right.

Alliances, Hybrids, and NGO Politics

Issue alliances, convergent advocacy campaigns, and hybrid NGOs are shifting the focus of the two fields. Leading NGOs in each sector—Oxfam, CARE, ActionAid, Amnesty, Human Rights First, OMCT, and others—are finding ways to broaden and deepen their sector-crossing agendas and methods, often in the aftermath of their participation in networks, alliances, and working groups involving both fields. These campaigns are important in their own right, but they are significant for two broader reasons as well: they call attention to issues of economic governance and corporate behavior—the "globalization" issues—in concrete, specific, and sometimes compelling ways; and they constitute an important new current in the politics of NGO advocacy that challenges prevailing themes in the scholarly debate over NGOs and their significance. We discuss this reframing of NGO advocacy and of social movement campaigns on globalization in the concluding chapter.

In an era of critiques of NGO advocacy, the new alliances and convergent campaigns need to be taken into account. The heroic aura that has surrounded international NGOs in some scholarship is provoking more critical examination of their record, including the extent to which they act independently of the major industrial country governments and aid agencies. Guilhot (2005) argues that human rights advocacy has morphed into an expertise-based form of democracy promotion under the control of the United States and international financial agencies. His concern that the guardians of human rights are being enlisted in a campaign to promote a democracy agenda defined too narrowly to serve the interests of poor-country governments and their citizens should be taken seriously. But the new rights advocacy movements analyzed here suggest that another important tendency is alive among international human rights NGOs, one that presents a more complex and alternative picture of the sector. In their work on agrarian reform, water privatization, HIV/AIDS, and other social policy issues, international NGOs are coming under pressure to form alliances with social movements and to reinforce their campaigning work by appealing to human rights standards and principles.

In the process they are often working against the current of the rich-country governments. This is particularly true for U.S.-based NGOs, as the U.S. government resists all appeals to economic and social rights as a basis for policy. But on issues involving water privatization and intellectual property rights over pharmaceuticals, many European governments have generally backed the claims of multinational pharmaceutical companies and of major Swiss, British, and French water multinationals, placing human rights advocates in opposition to corporate positions, prevailing interpretations of trade rules, and to governments' economic and trade policies. In economic and social policy areas, many international human rights and some development NGOs appear to be anything but the obedient agents of the G-8, fixed in opposition by their commitments to human rights standards and their alliances with social movements in the poor countries.

Issue alliances that involve both human rights and development advocates, campaigns that involve a convergence of objectives, strategies, and methods, and hybrid organizations in which the methods and cultures of the two fields are integrated have become an important part of the process in setting and implementing economic and social policy. The gradual intensification of human rights–development cooperation during campaigns on project-specific and issue-focused advocacy campaigns reflects both the heightened urgency that international NGOs feel about responding to conditions of poverty and the leading role that NGOs and movements based in the poor countries have played in driving that integration.

As international NGOs in human rights and development reposition themselves to engage in these social policy debates, they are caught up in new relationships and alliances and exposed to new methods and strategies that further change their historically distinct fields. The significance of these changes for the sectors themselves, their likely durability, their impact on social policy, and their importance for human rights and social theory are the subjects of the final chapter.

Notes

1. The sections on HIV/AIDS and water draw heavily on Nelson and Dorsey (2007).
2. See the investigative reports at www.hrw.org/doc/?t=hivaids&document_limit=0,2).

5

HUMAN RIGHTS
AND DEVELOPMENT
What Is New? Will It Last?

*F*ocusing on human freedoms contrasts with *narrower views of development, such as identifying development with the growth of gross national product, or with the rise in personal incomes. . . . Growth of GNP or of individual incomes can, of course, be very important as means to expanding the freedoms enjoyed by the members of society. But freedoms depend on other determinants, such as social and economic arrangements (for example for education and health care) as well as political and civil rights. . . . If freedom is what development advances, then there is a major argument for concentrating on that overarching objective, rather than on some particular means, or some specially chosen list of instruments.*

—Amartya Sen, *Development as Freedom*, 2000

The first decade of the twenty-first century is in many ways not a propitious time for an expanded human rights agenda. Some of the world's most powerful governments are violating fundamental human rights, resorting to torture and disregarding their obligations to ensure due process in their zeal to wage a "war" on terrorism and to protect themselves from potential threats. In so doing, they create a permissive culture for other governments to follow suit. But in a period that threatens human rights retrenchment, the quest for power, expanded influence, and ultimately efficacy against poverty and social

165

exclusion is driving the new rights advocacy. For development NGOs, business as usual has not produced changes in the level of suffering or conditions of poverty, and much of the human rights enterprise has come to believe that a comprehensive approach to human dignity that examines systems of inequality underlying oppressions is essential to stopping the tide of violence and protecting any rights.

The accounts of NGO activity found in the preceding pages—new coalitions and movements, organizational innovations, and human rights–based political strategies—are significant at several levels. The trends and movements discussed in these pages, among international NGOs in development and human rights and among movements and networks in the poor countries, are important to scholars of social movements and international relations because they suggest new ways to frame and theorize political activity in the international arena. They are significant for policymakers because they point to a set of international political actors asserting new rights and testing new strategies to influence policymakers' decisions and practices. They challenge corporations because they assert a guiding framework for what has sometimes been ad hoc and haphazard development of standards for corporate conduct, and they are significant to the NGOs themselves because they change the historic fields of development and human rights and set new organizational expectations.

But fundamentally, their importance is to the lives of large numbers of people who live under inhuman social, economic, and political conditions. Human rights and development NGOs exist, after all, to affirm, assert, uphold, and promote human dignity and human well-being, and debates over their strategies and methodologies should always be carried out with this broad shared mission in mind.

The inequality, deprivation, and marginalization that cloud the human condition are what motivates many of the strategic changes analyzed here and what makes the strategic choices of these NGOs worth studying. International development NGOs' move from framing their work as an expression of generosity to demanding that it be a response to universal standards and entitlements comes in large part out of a collective frustration at the inefficacy, or limited impact, of their best efforts to date to stem the rising tide of poverty. International human rights NGOs' decision to embrace economic and social rights also reflects the belief that the standards, norms, and vision that the sector upholds must be relevant and applicable to all dimensions of people's lives, that human dignity can be reduced neither to political and civil freedoms nor to material well-being.

This is why it is important for scholars to study the changing strategies of the human rights and development sectors. The strategic changes being undertaken carry great potential as well as grave risks; billions of dollars and enormous human energy and trust are placed in the hands of development and human rights NGOs by their donors and by the communities and movements that choose to ally with them. Because their formal accountability is less well-defined than that of states, they should be subject to the most rigorous independent efforts to monitor their work and assess their impact. If scholars and practitioners could mount a well-informed and systematic effort to assess the effectiveness and failings of new rights advocacy strategies, the intellectual gains and the benefits for human rights and human well-being could be enormous. Whether human rights and development are on the verge of a powerful new movement or on a slippery slope of rising rhetoric and declining rigor, careful scholarship has an important role to play in speaking the truth to those who challenge power.

In the remaining pages we address four questions: (a) what is new in the trends and movements discussed here; (b) in what senses and to what extent are the fields converging; (c) how durable are these changes in the human rights and development fields likely to be; and (d) what is their impact?

New economic and social rights agendas at the most influential international human rights NGOs; varied and tentative steps to implement rights-based development strategies among development organizations; and coalitions, alliances, and hybrid activist organizations linked to social movements: all these are signs of the expanded commitment to applying the logic and political power of human rights to economic and social policy.

The new rights advocacy is diverse, and not all of its dimensions are new or unanticipated. But the organizations and movements discussed here, including government agencies, international NGOs that are household names in many parts of the world, and specialized NGOs and social movements that may be little known outside of their fields, are collectively responding to rapid change in the international system and in their operating environments by seeking new sources of power and influence. When seen through the multiple lenses of social theory, international relations, human rights theory, and organizational theories, several new and important developments emerge that challenge contemporary practice in human rights and development and theories and models of international politics.

Within and among the human rights and development sectors we have documented a gradual increase in the level and intensity of cooperation, shared agendas, joint action, and (less frequently) adoption of shared methods. In local debates over major development projects, global meetings on social, environmental, and human rights policy, and in thematic advocacy campaigns on transnational policy issues, collaboration grew slowly in the early 1990s. Since then it has grown more rapidly as NGOs in both fields sought sources of leverage to challenge and regulate the growing power of transnational corporations or to subject national development policy decisions to public scrutiny and to the principles and standards of international human rights.

What Is New?

The new rights advocacy borrows methods drawn from the experience of civil and political rights advocacy, and many of its participants are veterans of advocacy on social policy, human rights, and environmental issues over two decades or more. But while there is important continuity in the story of human rights–development interaction, four major features and developments, outlined in chapter 1, set it apart from the patterns of previous NGO political action, and require our attention and reflection.

POWER, STRATEGIC ACTION, HUMAN RIGHTS, AND THE SECTORS

We have invoked the concept of power, and the varied postures of international NGOs toward power, in many parts of this account. NGOs invoke human rights in critical circumstances as a source of power, as a way of reframing a debate, as a tool for gaining legal and political leverage for resisting neoliberal economic norms and the dominance of intellectual property rights, and as a source of empowering concepts and language at the individual level. International NGOs, we posited in chapter 1, embrace human rights and broaden their human rights agendas because they are compelled to make strategic choices by changing international systems that dramatically affect their operating environment and require a response. They make these responses, in some cases, decisively enough to change the orientation not only of individual NGOs or programs but of the fields themselves.

NGOs and social movement organizations have adopted human rights strategies in response to the rapid rise of privatization of water utilities and the creation of new trade and intellectual property rules that restrict societies' ability to respond to critical public health threats, as well as in debates and battles over dam building, oil exploration, conscription of children, and agrarian reform. In the process, the human rights and development fields have begun to reorient and redefine themselves at the international level. The extent and limitations of this redefinition are further discussed below as an issue of convergence.

But to assume that NGOs are driven solely by these principled agendas would be too simplistic. NGOs, we have seen, also act to protect their own independence or appearance of independence, to sustain their reputations, and to protect their access to resources that are vital to their missions. Can we speak of this organizational behavior in terms of power? We argue that this organizational behavior, too, should be understood in terms of power, and that by doing so we can integrate understanding of organizational behavior with the political behavior of NGOs. NGOs' search for sources of power, in this sense, has been motivated both by the organizations' need to defend their own interests, as when international development NGOs shore up their independence from official donors by embracing human rights, and by the need for political leverage or traction in an effort to influence powerful institutions or entrenched policies, as in the choice of a human rights strategy to campaign for housing or access to essential medicines.

Often, these organizational and principled political objectives are difficult to disentangle. An important source of legitimacy for international NGOs, for example, is the credibility bestowed by the support and approval of dynamic movements and NGOs based in the countries of the global South. The persistent calls by movements and NGOs based in the poor countries for international human rights NGOs to embrace ESC rights agendas is important to the political power and agendas of the human rights movements, and it is also a source of organizational pressure for international NGO managers.

NEW CLAIMS AND NEW RIGHTS

How do new human rights arise, and what is their significance? Although we have not made the debate between social origins and legal-positivist views of human rights a central focus, we believe that the experiences of human rights, development, and social policymaking since the mid-1990s offer a clear perspective.

International human rights NGOs, as we have seen in chapter 2, have employed a succession of strategies in their efforts to address economic and social rights, and both fields have experienced a series of engagements with policy issues in which both human rights and development agencies have been involved. In many of these the assertion of new rights claims is linked to internationally recognized human rights standards, as in the cases of the right to water, right of access to essential medicines, or to agrarian reform.

Popular movements responding to globalization are increasingly attempting to apply the full range of human rights standards to economic, trade, and financial policy issues and to the regulation of corporate behavior. As Stammers (1999) has argued, human rights claims often arise in the context of social movement struggles and are a means of asserting or limiting political or economic power. Movements around trade, finance, and corporate social responsibility are asserting human rights as standards for regulating corporate conduct. This process of building the authority of human rights standards in economic and social issues parallels the assertion of civil and political rights by movements that began in earlier decades against torture, disappearances, and denial of civil rights. Whether new rights become legally codified or subsequently litigated is a test of the degree of adoption at the international level.

In addition to seeking leverage over international corporate activity, activists are reframing what was once identified as the "antiglobalization" movement to one that takes human rights standards and principles seriously in governing international economic and social affairs. Human rights are invoked sometimes for their international legal force, as in deliberations over TRIPs and licensing generic antiretroviral production, but more often to buttress domestic legal claims and to give moral and political support to social movement demands.

Exactly what is new in these cases varies, as do their origins. The human right to water became salient because of unprecedented, large-scale plans to change the terms of control of water supply systems and to alter drastically the quality of and access to water for citizen-consumers. The right to access to essential medicines became visible and entered public debates with the HIV/AIDS pandemic, the creation of new trade and intellectual property rules governing patents on drugs, and the growing cost and demand for other relatively expensive medicines to treat, for example, drug-resistant strains of tuberculosis.

Social movements and sometimes governments have asserted or "claimed" these rights and brought them into prominent places in international policy debates. But while the political power of human rights standards came in part from their social origins and their power to mobilize social movements, the political and legal leverage they have afforded in shaping international policy or action has depended profoundly on their status as internationally recognized legal standards in human rights covenants and treaties and on the skilled interpretation and application of those standards in particular situations.

What is new, then, is sometimes the content of the right (water), but more often the popular assertion of the right and the new forms of action for the right's defense and promotion. The conclusion is inescapable, we argue, that rights claims have risen powerfully out of concrete social situations and social movements. It is equally clear that for economic and social rights, their legal standing and the social mobilizations they help to frame and motivate have interacted powerfully to create new rights, new understandings of their implications, new strategies and arenas for their promotion and defense, and new language for their promotion by NGOs outside of the historic human rights field.

ACCOUNTABILITY AND PATTERNS OF NGO–STATE INTERACTION

International NGO advocacy on human rights and on the environment has historically often been an exercise in restricting or regulating state options: forcing compliance with environmental standards, challenging press censorship or arbitrary detentions, or insisting on greater transparency.[1] But the exercise of power need not mean placing limits on the state. Many of the cases discussed here involve international NGOs directly targeting corporate behavior or influencing international rulemaking to preserve or enlarge the policy options available to poor-country governments.

They enter into more complex relationships with poor-country governments, sometimes adversarial and sometimes supportive, and they assign responsibility for the failure to fulfill rights to multiple actors, often including powerful governments or international agencies. In some cases, new rights advocacy demands an accounting of the finance, trade, and development assistance policies of G-8 countries and their impact on economic and social rights. This discussion focuses on patterns and models of politics surrounding human rights

in poor countries, in keeping with our interest in the development–
human rights nexus. But human rights violations and activism are vi-
tally important and painfully real in wealthy, industrialized countries
as well. Human rights advocacy on the civil and political rights of persons detained in the United States, the United Kingdom, and elsewhere during investigations of potential terrorist threats continues to
focus largely on human rights as restraints on state behavior. And the
new movement for ESC rights in the United States explicitly stands in
solidarity with poor peoples' movements in the poor countries, demanding government and corporate accountability for their human
rights impacts.

NGO advocates often adopt a broad, two-pronged position: that
governments should retain more discretion in making choices regarding their trade and social policies; and that wealthy donor governments and international institutions should uphold their obligations
for international cooperation and assistance to advance ESC rights
in poor countries. This agenda implicitly broadens accountability,
shifting from a sole focus on the "violating state" and assigning responsibility to the actors that may create obstacles to the fulfillment
of human rights in a global economy. In their advocacy, NGOs are
striving to give concrete meaning to the concept of international accountability for ESC rights within poor countries, embedded in Article 2 of the International Covenant on Economic, Social, and
Cultural Rights (ICESCR).

Poor-country governments, of course, remain obligated to respect,
protect, and fulfill economic and social rights. International standards
emphasize states' duties to realize those rights and to ensure that they
are delivered without discrimination. The politics of human rights is
now "beyond the violating state" not because states are no longer accountable for fulfilling ESC rights, but because in a global economy
accountability is increasingly shared by corporations, international
economic actors, and in some cases rich-donor governments.

New rights advocacy addresses a broad range of issues, in diverse
political arenas (national and international), by "targeting" intergovernmental, governmental, and corporate actors, and it works through

a wide range of coalitions and partnerships. These place NGOs and social movements in a new posture as they attempt to establish the authority of human rights standards, including ESC rights, over social and economic policymaking.

We have profiled two of the principal social policy debates in contemporary international affairs: the privatization of water systems and the response to the global AIDS pandemic. Like other advocacy campaigns, such as those for access to essential medicines, for the right to agrarian reform, for women's property rights, and for the right to education, they exemplify the central characteristics of the new rights advocacy: the increasing specificity with which ESC rights are applied to social policy, international NGOs' complex relations with governments and international agencies, their appeal to human rights standards as a source of leverage against norms of liberalization and privatization, and the wide range of issues, strategies, and political arenas they address. Both cases originate with initiatives by local social movements determined to change, or prevent changes in, state policy.

The political environment in which ESC rights advocacy takes place puts advocates in a different relation to poor-country governments and to sources of political leverage in the international political arena. At times they oppose and condemn the violating state, at other times they attempt to shift responsibility for violations to the international level and onto economic actors. This is a new and distinct pattern of political action; rather than appealing to norms whose resonance is stronger in international arenas than in the target government, much ESC rights advocacy appeals to human rights standards that have stronger support in the countries of the global South. It reinforces their sovereignty rather than challenging it, and it applies the leverage derived from international human rights to limiting the influence of international actors.

This form of NGO politics differs from the boomerang model that is widely used in international relations. Fulfilling economic and social rights may involve reinforcing international norms while also calling for greater freedom for national governments and societies to set social policies. These advocacy strategies do not signal a whole-sale reversal by NGOs, which still call for stronger international regulation of child labor, natural resource management, labor rights, and others. But the new rights advocacy does represent a significant shift toward a more complex and varied relationship between international NGOs and poor-country governments, in which international NGOs often strategically support and cooperate with national authorities.

HUMAN RIGHTS CHALLENGING NEOLIBERAL DEVELOPMENT NORMS

New rights advocacy addresses policy issues in which a well-established set of neoliberal economic norms have dominated since the 1980s. NGO campaigning against neoliberal policies is not new, but the effective and issue-specific mobilization of human rights principles and standards against this dominant and controversial set of norms is new. Early efforts to promote civil and political rights confronted the competing (and dominant) norm of sovereignty, and advances in civil and political rights have often involved establishing the principle that human rights agreements give states the authority and the duty to investigate, comment on, and intervene in the relations of sovereign governments and their citizens.

Critics of structural adjustment and of debt burdens on poor-country governments have invoked human rights in the past, but the movements studied here are making their case with greater relevance to specific policy decisions. The right to health, for example, is also mobilized in support of a campaign for the right of access to essential medicines, in particular generically produced antiretrovirals. The right to food becomes the basis for a campaign for agrarian reform in the work of FIAN and has been directly marshaled in support of land occupations in Brazil organized under the Movimento dos Trabalhadores Rurais Sem Terra (MST). Similarly, international human rights NGOs now focus attention on property and inheritance rights of African women, which are foundational to housing rights and livelihoods.

But the challenge posed by the new rights advocacy to orthodox development models is most significant because it is not simply a critique, but an alternative. The alternative framework it advances is first a set of standards and principles against which all development policies are to be tested and assessed, and a normative framework that converts development cooperation from acts of generosity to human rights obligations. The challenge for development assistance, for the governance of trade, and for the crafting of national and local development strategies is to test every initiative and every planning process against standards that are not simply "best practice" for public officials or development professionals, but binding international obligations that are grounded in humanity's best effort at a common understanding of what human dignity requires.

Winning greater acceptance of the norms and principles of the full range of international human rights, it seems, is not an abstract debate carried out solely in UN committees and commissions, but an intensely political and diffuse national and local process in which the concerted, consistent, and sometimes coordinated claims of particular human rights build familiarity, legitimacy, and confidence in these rights as human rights. This confidence, in turn, is encouraging social movements and NGOs to use and claim these rights to influence decisions large and small, from constitutions to annual budgets and program priorities.

Are the Sectors Converging?

In chapter 1 we hypothesized that international systems changes were producing changes in NGOs' operating environment powerful enough to force strategic choices that could reorient not only single organizations, but the sectors. We have referred occasionally to a human rights–development "convergence," in reference to the increasing contact, collaboration, and joint action among human rights and development NGOs. We use the term largely to refer to any shifts toward shared or common methods, strategies, initiatives, and identities, but in its full sense, "convergence" is a daunting and risky prospect. If, in responding to rapid economic and political change and to the demands and models of NGO colleagues in the poor countries, the organizations of the human rights field fully embrace a role in mobilizing human rights against poverty and social exclusions, will the field lose its distinctive identity? Will Amnesty International USA, for example, draw so close to Oxfam America as to become indistinguishable by its constituents? Will the "brand" appeal and recognition of specialized organizations such as MSF and Physicians for Human Rights be diminished? More seriously, will the idea of human rights, built for decades in the West overwhelmingly around civil and political freedoms, become confused and weakened for the citizens whose support the movement seeks?

The forms of movement toward "convergence" that we have found do not seem to signal this kind of merging and blurring of identities and methods. The clearest evidence of movement toward convergence by the traditional international NGOs in the two fields are in the tactics of some development organizations and the shift of substantive issue agendas for many human rights NGOs. Oxfam's global advocacy, for example, makes tactical use of human rights rhetorical appeals in addressing the pharmaceutical industry, CARE draws on human rights principles in its analysis of poverty and program design, and Save the Children is pressing for a more direct reference to human rights standards for children among many of its national affiliates.

For human rights organizations, it is the content of their agendas that gives the clearest evidence of movement toward the development sector, with growing work on corporate conduct and labor standards, defense of environmental, AIDS, and labor activists, and work on food, health, housing, and other sectors. As the collective agenda of international human rights NGOs broadens to include more attention to the full range of rights of poor and marginalized people, significant changes in methodology may eventually follow. But to date, traditional human rights methods have prevailed. Human Rights Watch chooses ESC rights issues that suit its research methodology, and Human Rights First's methodology of partnership work is not fundamentally changed. At Amnesty International, the methods by which the movement will work on ESC rights campaigns are still parallel to and consistent with those employed for civil and political rights advocacy, but if Amnesty International infuses rights into its campaigning as fully as anticipated, it may alter its methods over time. Whether these changes alter the perceptions of its constituents or the general public is another matter.

Only in a handful of hybrid organizations do we observe a blending of the core methods of the fields. Human rights NGOs have not taken up delivering direct assistance or community development work, nor have established development NGOs begun any systematic use of human rights documentation, reporting, or litigation. The worries of some human rights activists that the field might lose its clear identity in expanding and deepening its ESC rights agenda do not seem to be justified by the pattern of organizational change we have observed.

Beyond the NGO and United Nations agencies, the professional and academic boundaries between the fields are still seldom traversed. Research on human rights–based development is almost completely dominated by practitioners active in the field or situated in specialized think tanks such as the Oxford-based International NGO Training and Research Centre. There will continue to be a real need to document and evaluate these substantial changes in the human rights and development fields. Further research on the institutional relationship between the fields should also track the development of academic and professional centers of training and research.

Durability

Are the trends detailed here lasting, durable changes to the development and human rights fields, or are they fads, fashions that rise for a decade and recede into memory or are absorbed into a kind of global business as usual? Predicting the future is risky business, and we are wary of extending our analysis into the unknown. But if the past and the shape of organizational behavior in the two sectors can be reliable guides, then it is possible to make some informed projections and pinpoint key actors to watch in assessing the impact of changes in development and human rights.

We argued in chapter 1 that the two sectors have historically different tendencies, conditioned by the fact that human rights advocates have been more strongly and consistently united in an adversarial effort to establish the authority of internationally recognized human rights standards and principles over states, while international development NGOs have often been more cooperative with the state and less united as a sector of organizations. One result is that the movement to adopt ESC rights as a source of power and leverage is clearer and more decisive among human rights NGOs. Among international development NGOs, rights-based approaches remain a countercurrent to the mainstream in the field. How enduring will the trends be in individual organizations and in the sectors?

International human rights NGOs' new commitments have been made in the context of a growing global movement for ESC rights, especially in the poor countries, and would be difficult to reverse. Any step by the major international NGOs to retreat entirely to a civil and political rights–focused agenda would be interpreted as backing away from conditions of widespread abuse and denial of economic and social human rights, as well as from the expressed concerns of many colleague organizations around the world, and would carry a high cost for unity, trust, and cooperation among human rights advocates worldwide. Such a move would open NGOs to criticism for bifurcating rights and undercutting the core concepts of indivisibility, as governments did in the cold war era. The degree to which economic and social rights will be effectively integrated in organizational agendas and in public conceptions of human rights remains to be seen, but the direction of the movement is clear.

The future course of rights-based development approaches is harder to project. International human rights NGOs are, in a sense, embracing a long-neglected and coequal part of the existing legal structure of human rights, but in development the move to embrace human rights is more voluntary and tactical, not completing an incomplete agenda for the sector, but seizing an opportunity to reframe key development issues, refurbish organizational images, or both. Organizations such as Oxfam and ActionAid that have made widespread commitments to colleague and partner NGOs would find it difficult directly to renounce or retreat from rights-based approaches, but in development, the language of the rights-based approach can be made to coexist rhetorically with human needs, charity, human development, and the Millennium Development Goals. The development industry has a history of absorbing new rhetorical and conceptual frameworks into a patchwork of approaches.

ESC rights advocates' greatest challenge may be that the rights they advocate confront well-established norms of a market-oriented development paradigm, against which NGO advocates had little success in the 1980s and 1990s. Research is needed to test the impact of ESC rights over the coming decade by monitoring the strategies and impact of advocacy, especially on issues that directly confront norms and practices of liberalization, privatization, and unregulated free trade. Research and impact evaluations should aim to assess whether ESC rights advocacy can, in fact, "mobilize shame" and generate public pressure sufficient to impact donor country policies or international regimes.

Whether such advocacy strategies can succeed, and to what extent, without significant support from the U.S. government or the most influential international organizations remains to be seen. The answer is likely to depend heavily on two considerations: whether significant constituencies can be built globally, and whether a compelling case can be made that human rights–based approaches yield superior social and human results in health, education, gender equity, and nutrition. The record of human rights–based advocacy on social and economic policy suggests that broad and diverse configurations of participants can be expected. The partially successful experience of HIV/AIDS activists at the November 2001 Doha WTO Round suggests that support from social movements based in industrial countries may be a key political ingredient. Medical professionals, HIV/AIDS activists, human rights NGOs, and international public health advocates all participated in the WTO effort.

Demonstrating impact on key social indicators will also be key to winning institutional support among major development funders. There has been progress here on several fronts toward sets of indicators that operationalize ESC rights (Hertel 2006), including the 2005 *Manual* on the environment and human rights produced by the Science and Human Rights Project of the American Association for the Advancement of Science, and work is now under way at the Center for Economic and Social Rights to develop ESC rights–specific indicators.

But the Millennium Development Goals offer the greatest resource for developing widely accepted standards. The MDGs' goals and indicators, with their focus on quick-impact strategies that promise immediate statistical impact, appear to have become the focal point of UN and most bilateral donors' discourse and programming on poverty, even though they have gained limited traction with social movements and NGOs in the poor countries (Nelson 2007). But the indicators and data collection systems that track progress toward the MDGs are the best and most widely recognized system available for monitoring social indicators for many ESC rights standards.

The MDGs could underscore and reinforce the rights-based approach if they were tied strongly to human rights standards in promotion and implementation efforts by UN agencies and other donors. But for the most part they are not closely linked. Donors avoid the responsibilities and accountability that come with human rights, and a concerted effort is needed to ensure that the MDGs do not draw attention away from rights-based approaches rather than reinforce them.

Impact on Outcomes

After forty years of relative quiet from the mainstream international human rights NGOs on economic and social issues, and decades of near-silence from the development sector on the subject of economic and social rights standards, it is still early to reach meaningful conclusions about the bottom line: what impact will the new rights advocacy have on policy outcomes and the well-being of groups whose rights have been so systematically neglected and denied?

At the agency level, national level, and global level there are some indications of the political and institutional situations in which the new rights advocacy may be most—and least—effective. At the national level, in a country such as South Africa, where ESC rights standards have been embraced and affirmed clearly and strongly in the country's constitution, rights-based advocacy on health, water, and land issues appears to have real political traction. Advocates have won significant policy changes and commitments by pressing their case, as with the Treatment Action Campaign, in moral and rights terms. Advocates for the right to water have won victories in the South African courts and in municipal councils as well. Invoking rights, even when it succeeds in changing policy, does not solve resource constraints, and the difficulty of financing national health and HIV/AIDS treatment commitments is limiting the visible short-term impact of South Africa's new policies.

In other settings, invoking social rights such as the right to water has proven effective in mobilizing resistance to privatization, to blocking or delaying the feared transformation of water service from public utility to private business. Human rights strategies have helped promote and defend landless peoples' occupations of underused land in Brazil and elsewhere, and human rights strategies have succeeded in clarifying the policy and funding implications of housing rights and education rights elsewhere.

In general, there is clearer evidence of the power of human rights to motivate and mobilize resistance to privatization, and to policy change, than of its ability to press governments to provide services more equitably, adequately, and effectively. Put differently, we have found considerable evidence that new rights campaigns can effectively encourage states to protect the right to water or to education from disruption by privatization schemes or prepayment mechanisms with arbitrary service cutoffs, and encourage governments to respect economic and social rights by refraining from levying prohibitive school or health care fees or from denying access to unused land.

Success in pressing for fulfillment of these rights is—to date—more difficult to find. International sources of finance will almost certainly have to play a role if governments in Africa, most of Latin America, and Asia are to move from eliminating arbitrary barriers to creating systems—likely involving market, state, and voluntary mechanisms—that actually enable citizens to enjoy these rights.

One important strategy for researchers will be to see, in countries and municipalities where water privatization has been rejected, whether human rights advocates can also use their moral and legal power to bring about improvements in state-managed utilities. Other research priorities remain as well, particularly to identify and analyze more clearly the major trends that shape human rights strategies, to examine closely the implications for individual organizations of the strategic shifts we have observed, and to monitor closely the impact of human rights–driven strategies on national and subnational policy outcomes and impacts. What are the practical and specific requirements, in staffing, information, fundraising, training, and education, of adopting rights-based approaches in development and ESC rights agendas in human rights? Are outcomes of development policies in health, nutrition, education, or employment more favorable or less favorable in settings where human rights–based activism and monitoring is prominent? Can market-based provision of goods such as water be coupled with human rights–based guarantees and regulation in ways that take advantage of market efficiencies without compromising the integrity of human rights or the well-being of individuals? Has progress toward specific MDG targets been more in evidence where the goals and benchmarks are linked to human rights guarantees and backed by rights-based advocacy?

There is no shortage of questions for a research agenda that pursues the changes occurring in the development and human rights sectors. Questions, whether framed around theoretical debates or driven by an interest in outcomes, can help scholars and practitioners to clarify the risks and likely benefits of strategic responses to change in the global economy and in national societies. Such research, like the strategic choices of state and nongovernmental agencies, is also a high-stakes activity, as the research will assess the impacts of NGO strategies in this realm and may define their viability in the future. The choices that NGOs and other agencies make, and the information on which those choices are based, will be visible in patterns of policy and practice, change and resistance to change, that shape the prospects of the world's poorest, most disenfranchised and vulnerable people, and, through them, prospects for peaceful and replicable solutions to vexing social problems.

Note

1. This section and the one that follows, on challenges to neoliberal development models, draw heavily on Nelson and Dorsey (2007).

Bibliography

ActionAid. 2005. Rights to End Poverty. On file with the authors.

ActionAid India. 2006. Reaching the Unreached. *Rights First. Newsletter of Action Aid India* www.actionaidindia.org/download/AAInewsletter.pdf (accessed on July 6, 2006).

Aguirre, Iñaque. 2005. Social Investigation of the Communities Affected by the Chixoy Dam. *International Rivers Network*. www.irn.org/pdf/chixoy/ChixoyLegacy.2005/vol4.01-03.pdf (accessed on September 22, 2006).

Aguirre, Monti. 2004. The Chixoy Dam Destroyed Our Lives. Human Rights Dialogue. *Environmental Rights* (Spring).

Ahmed, Karim, Anya Ferring, and Lina Ibarra Ruiz. 2005. Manual on Environmental Health Indicators and Benchmarks: Human Rights Perspectives. Program on Science and Human Rights. Washington, D.C.: American Association for the Advancement of Science.

Alsop, R. 2005. *Power, Rights and Poverty: Concepts and Connections*. Washington, D.C.: World Bank.

Alston, Philip. 1998. Making Space for Human Rights: The Case of the Right to Development. *Harvard Human Rights Yearbook* 1, no. 1.

Alston, Philip, and Mary Robinson, eds. 2005. *Human Rights and Development: Towards Mutual Reinforcement*. Oxford: Oxford University Press.

Ambler, John. 2002. The Program Strategy Paper: A Tool for Integrating CARE's Household Livelihood Survey and the Rights-Based Approaches. Internal CARE document. On file with the authors.

Amenga-Etego, Rudolf, and Sara Grusky. 2005. The New Face of Conditionalities: The World Bank and Water Privatization in Ghana. In *The Age of Commodity; Water Privatization in Southern Africa*, ed. David A. McDonald and Greg Ruiters, 275–90. London: Earthscan.

Amnesty International, 1998. Chad: Freedom of Expression Again under Attack. August 3, 1998. www.amnesty.org/library/Index/ENGAFR 200091998?open&of=ENG-TCD

———. 2001. *Annual Report*. http://web.amnesty.org/report2001

———. 2003. World Water Forum. On file with authors.

———. 2004a. Guatemala: Human Rights Defenders at Risk. AI Index AMR 34/019/2004. http://www.amnestyusa.org/countries/guatemala/document.do?id=ENGAMR340162006 (accessed on September 22, 2006).

———. 2004b. Nigeria: Are Human Rights in the Pipeline? http://web.amnesty.org/library/Index/ENGAFR440202004 (accessed on September 22, 2006).

———. 2005a. Report 2005: The State of the World's Human Rights. AI Index: POL 10/001/2005. http://web.amnesty.org/report2005/index-eng

———. 2005b. Human Rights and Human Dignity: A Primer on Economic, Social and Cultural Rights. Amnesty International.

———. 2006. HIV and AIDS: A Human Rights Based Approach; to HIV and AIDS. http://www.amnestyusa.org/hiv_aids/index.do (accessed on September 22, 2006).

Amnesty International United Kingdom and The International Business Leaders Forum. 2002. Business and Human Rights: A Geography of Corporate Risk. www.iblf.org/resources/general.jsp?id=69 (accessed on September 22, 2006).

Amnesty International USA. n.d. Just Earth? Chad-Cameroon. www.amnestyusa.org/justearth/chad-cameroon.html (accessed September 22, 2006).

Anheier, Helmut, Marlies Glasius, and Mary Kaldor, eds. 2004. *Global Civil Society 2004/5.* London: Sage.

Anti-Privatisation Forum. 2003. The Struggle against Pre-Paid Water Meters in Soweto. 10 September 2003, at www.labournet.net/world/0309/sawater1.html

Arbour, L. 2005. Freedom from Want—From Charity for Entitlement. Speech for the LaFontaine-Baldwin Award 2005. http://citoyen.onf.ca/extraits/media/lecture_arbour_an.pdf

———. 2006. Using Human Rights to Reduce Poverty, *Development Outreach: Human Rights and Development* 1, no. 1 (October), at www1.worldbank.org/devoutreach/october06/article.asp?id=379

AWID. 2006. *Achieving Women's Economic and Social Rights: Strategies and Lessons from Experience.* Toronto: Association for Women's Rights in Development.

Bank Information Center and Catholic Relief Services. 2005. *Chad's Oil: Miracle or Mirage? Following the Money in Africa's Newest Petro-State.* Washington, D.C.: Bank Information Center.

Bank Information Center, Friends of the Earth, Environmental Defense, and Oxfam International. 2005. *Chad's Oil Revenue Management Experiment in Crisis*. Washington, D.C.: Bank Information Center.

Bannon, I., and P. Collier, eds. 2003. *Natural Resources and Violent Conflict— Options and Actions*. Washington D.C.: The World Bank.

Barnett, Michael, and Raymond Duvall. 2005. Power in International Politics. *International Organization* 59 (Winter): 39–75.

Barrow, Ondine, and Michael Jennings. 2001. *The Charitable Impulse: NGOs and Development in East and North-East Africa*. Oxford and Bloomfield, Conn.: James Curry and Kumarian.

Bendana, Alejandro. 2004. NGOs and Social Movements: A North-South Divide? at www.transcend.org/t_database/articles.php?ida=515 (accessed on September 15, 2006).

Berkman, Alan. 2001. The Global AIDS Crisis: Human Rights, International Pharmaceutical Markets and Intellectual Property Symposium. Remarks at the University of Connecticut Law School. December 2001. www .globaltreatmentaccess.org/content/press_releases/02/031402_HGAP _ALAN_PP_IPR.pdf (accessed on May 14, 2004).

Blue Planet Project. 2001. The Treaty Initiative to Share and Protect the Global Commons. June 14, 2001. www.waterobservatory.org (accessed on January 21, 2003).

Bob, Clifford. 2001. Marketing Rebellion: Insurgent Groups, International Media and NGO Support. *International Politics* 38, no. 3 (September).

———. 2005. *The Marketing of Rebellion: Insurgents, Media, and International Activism*. Cambridge: Cambridge University Press.

Bode, Brigitta, Jay Goulden, Francis Lwanda, and Elisa Martinez. 2005. Putting Rights-Based Development into Context: CARE's Programming Approaches in Malawi and Bangladesh. www.sed.manchester.ac.uk/ idpm/research/events/february2005/documents/Goulden.pdf (accessed on September 18, 2006).

Boli, John, and George Thomas, eds. 1999. *Constructing World Culture: International Non Governmental Organizations Since 1875*. Stanford, Calif.: Stanford University Press.

Browne, Stephen. 2000. *Beyond Aid: From Patronage to Partnership*. London: Ashgate.

Bryer, David, and Edmund Cairns. 1994. For Better? For Worse? Humanitarian Aid in Conflict. *Development in Practice* 7, no. 4: 363–74.

Brysk, Alison. 2005. *Human Rights and Private Wrongs: Constructing Global Civil Society*. New York: Routledge.

Buzan, Barry, and Richard Little. 1994. The Idea of "International System": Theory Meets History. *International Political Science Review* 15, no. 3: 231–55.

Cabinet of the Republic of South Africa. 2003. Cabinet statement on treat-plan for HIV and AIDS. www.gcis.gov.za/media/cabinet/031119.htm

Campbell, John L. 2005. Where Do We Stand? Common Mechanisms in Organizations and Social Movement Research. In *Social Movements and Organization Theory*, ed. Gerald F. Davis et. al, 41–68. Cambridge: Cambridge University Press.

CARE. 2005. Principles into Practice: Learning from Innovative Rights-based Programmes. www.careinternational.org.uk/Principles%20into%20 practice%3A%20Learning%20from%20innovative%20rights-based%20programmes+6216.twl (accessed November 26, 2007).

———. 2006. Care's Activities and Initiatives on Inclusive and Democratic Governance. www.caresa-lesotho.org.za/activities4.htm (accessed on May 28, 2006).

CARE International. 2003. *CARE's Experience with Adoption of a Rights-based Approach, Five Case Studies.* Internal report. On file with the authors.

CARE International UK. 2005. Principles into Practice. Learning from Innovative Rights-Based Programmes. www.careinternational.org.uk/?lid=6215 (accessed on January 28, 2008).

Carothers, Thomas. 2000. Civil Society. *Foreign Policy* (Winter).

Catholic Relief Services, n.d. Our Work, Cameroon. www.crs.org/our_work/where_we_work/overseas/africa/cameroon/ (accessed on September 21, 2006).

Catsam, Marcus, and Danika Kazmer. 2003. *UNDP and the Rights-Based Approach.* Unpublished typescript on file with the authors.

Center for Economic and Social Rights. 2001. Right to Water Fact Sheet #1: Global Statistics. www.cesr.org/filestore2/download/116 (accessed on November 24, 2007).

Centre on Housing Rights and Evictions (COHRE). 2004a. *Guatemala: The Chixoy Dam Case. Petition Submitted by the Centre on Housing Rights and Evictions on Behalf of the Survivors of the Rio Negro Community and Similarly Situated Communities in Guatemala.* Geneva: COHRE.

———. 2004b. *Mission Report—Continuing the Struggle for Justice and Accountability in Guatemala: Making Reparations a Reality in the Chixoy Dam Case.* Geneva: COHRE.

———. 2004c. *Legal Resources for the Right to Water: International and National Standards.* COHRE Sources No. 8. Geneva: COHRE.

Clark, Ann Marie. 1995. Non Governmental Organizations and Their Influence on International Society. *Journal of International Affairs* 48, no. 2: 507–25.

———. 2001. *Diplomacy of Conscience: Amnesty International and Changing Human Rights Norms.* Princeton, N.J.: Princeton University Press.

Committee on Economic, Social and Cultural Rights. 2002. General Comment 15: The Right to Water. www.waterobservatory.org/library/uploadedfiles/right_to_water_Articles_11_and_12_of_the_Inter.pdf (accessed on June 6, 2007).

Conca, Ken. 2005. *Governing Water: Contentious Transnational Politics and Global Institution Building.* Cambridge, Mass.: MIT Press.

Concannon, Tim, and Hannah Griffiths. 2001. Stealing our Water: Implications of GATS for Global Water Resources www.foodfirst.org/progs/global/trade/wto2001/stealingwater.html (accessed on May 14, 2004).

Darrow, Mac, and Tomas Amparo. 2005. Power, Capture and Conflict: A Call for Human Rights Accountability in Development Cooperation. *Human Rights Quarterly* 27: 471–538.

Della Porta, Donatella, and Sidney Tarrow, eds. 2005. *Transnational Protest and Global Activism: People, Passions and Power.* Lanham, Md.: Rowman and Littlefield.

DFID. 2000. *Realizing Human Rights for Poor People: Strategies for Achieving the International Development Targets.* London: DFID. On file with authors.

Dichter, Thomas W. 2001. *Despite Good Intentions: Why Development Assistance to the Third World Has Failed.* Amherst: University of Massachusetts Press.

Dimaggio, Paul J., and Walter W. Powell. 1983. The Iron Cage Revisited: Institutional Isomorphism and Collective Rationality in Organizational Fields. *American Sociological Review* 48: 147–60.

Donnelly, Elizabeth A. 2002. Proclaiming Jubilee: The Debt and Structural Adjustment Network, in *Restructuring World Politics: Transnational Social Movements, Networks and Norms,* ed. Sanjeev Khagram, James V. Riker, and Kathryn Sikkink, 155–80. Minneapolis: University of Minnesota Press.

Doperak, Beth, and Shawna Szabo. 2003. *Oxfam Great Britain: A Partner Analysis.* Unpublished typescript, on file with authors.

Dorsey, Ellen. 1992. Expanding the Foreign Policy Discourse: Transnational Social Movements and the Globalization of Citizenship. In *The Limits of State Autonomy: Societal Groups and Foreign Policy Formulation,* ed. David Skidmore and Valerie Hudson. Boulder, Colo.: Westview Press.

————. 1996. The Global Women's Movement: Towards a New Model of Global Governance. In *Politics and Global Governance*, ed. Paul Diehl. Boulder, Colo.: Lynne Rienner Publishers.

————. 2000. US Policy and Human Rights NGOs: New Challenges in the Global Era. In *The United States and Human Rights: Looking Inward and Outward*, ed. David Forsythe. Lincoln: University of Nebraska Press.

————. 2002. Root Causes to Full Spectrum: Human Rights and Development Organizations Confront Economic Globalization. Paper presented at the International Studies Association, New Orleans, 2002.

Drinan, Robert F. 2001. *The Mobilization of Shame*. New Haven, Conn.: Yale University Press.

EarthRights International. 2004. Mining, Gender and the Environment in Burma. www.earthrights.org/burmareports/mining_gender_and_the_environment_in_burma.html (accessed on August 2, 2005).

————. n.d. EarthRights International, What We Do. www.earthrights.org/about_us.html (accessed on September 22, 2006).

Ebrahim, Alnoor, 2005. Accountability Myopia: Losing Sight of Organizational Learning. *Nonprofit and Voluntary Sector Quarterly* 34, no. 1: 56–897.

Edwards, Michael. 1998. International Development NGO's: Agents of Foreign Aid or Vehicles of International Co-operation. *Discourse: A Journal of Policy Studies* (Summer).

————. 2000. *NGO Rights and Responsibilities: A New Deal for Global Governance*. London: Foreign Policy Centre.

Edwards, Michael, and John Gaventa, eds. 2001. *Global Citizen Action*. Boulder, Colo.: Lynne Rienner Publishers.

Environmental Defense, Bank Information Center, Catholic Relief Services. 2004. *The Chad-Cameroon Pipeline: The Case for Implementation of the EIR Recommendations*. Washington, D.C.: Environmental Defense.

Escobar, A. 1995. *Encountering Development: The Making and Unmaking of the Third World*. Princeton, N.J.: Princeton University Press.

Falk, Richard A. 2000. *Human Rights Horizons: The Pursuit of Justice in a Globalizing World*. New York: Routledge.

Ferguson, James. 1990. *The Anti-Politics Machine: "Development," Depoliticization, and Bureaucratic Power in Lesotho*. Cambridge: Cambridge University Press.

Fisher, Julie. 1993. *The Road from Rio: Sustainable Development and the Non Governmental Movement in the Third World*. Westport, Conn.: Praeger Publishers.

Florini, Ann M, ed. 2000. *The Third Force: The Rise of Transnational Civil Society.* Tokyo and Washington, D.C.: Japan Center for International Exchange and the Carnegie Endowment for International Peace.

Forsythe, David P. 1997. The United Nations, Human Rights and Development. *Human Rights Quarterly* 19, no. 2: 334–49.

———. 2000. *Human Rights in International Relations.* Cambridge: Cambridge University Press.

———. 2005. *The Humanitarians: The International Committee of the Red Cross.* Cambridge: Cambridge University Press.

Fowler, Alan. 1997. *Striking a Balance: A Guide to Enhancing the Effectiveness of Non-governmental Organizations in International Development.* London: Earthscan.

———. 2000a. Beyond Partnership. *IDS Bulletin* 31, no. 3 (July): 1–13.

———. 2000b. *The Virtuous Spiral: A Guide to Sustainability for NGOs in International Development.* London: Earthscan.

Fox, Jonathan, and L. David Brown. 1998. *The Struggle for Accountability.* Cambridge, Mass.: MIT Press.

Frankovitz, Andre. 2002. Rules to Live By: The Human Rights Approach to Development. *Praxis* 17: 1–14.

Friedman, Elisabeth J. 2003. Gendering the Agenda: The Impact of the Transnational Women's Rights Movement at the UN Conferences of the 1990s. *Women's Studies International Forum* 26, no. 4: 313–31.

Friedman, Elisabeth J., Kathryn Hochstetler, and Anne Marie Clark. 2005. *Sovereignty, Democracy, and Global Civil Society: State-Society Relations at UN World Conferences.* Albany: State University of New York Press.

Friedman, Stephen, and Shauna Mottiar. 2005. A Rewarding Engagement? The Treatment Action Campaign and the Politics of HIV/AIDS. *Politics and Society* 33, no. 4: 511–65.

Friends of the Earth–Japan. 2005. Letter to Mr. James Wolfensohn, President, The World Bank. March 14, 2005. www.environmentaldefense.org/documents/4369_NGO%20letterNT2Laos.pdf

Gauri, Varun. 2004. Social Rights and Economics: Claims to Health Care and Education in Developing Countries. *World Development* 32, no. 3: 465–77.

Ghana National Coalition against the Privatisation of Water. 2001. Accra Declaration on the Right to Water. www.isodec.org.gh/Papers/accradeclaration.PDF (accessed on February 6, 2006).

Global Committee for the Water Contract. 1998. The Water Manifesto. www.gdrc.org/uem/water/WATER_MANIFESTO.doc (accessed November 25, 2007).

Globalization Challenge Initiative. 2001. Water Privatization in Ghana? An Analysis of Government and World Bank Policies. www.servicesforall .org/ (accessed on January 29, 2006).

Goldman, Michael. 2005. *Imperial Nature: The World Bank and Struggles for Social Justice in the Age of Globalization.* New Haven, Conn.: Yale University Press.

Golub, Stephen. 2005. Less Law and Reform, More Politics and Enforcement: A Civil Society Approach to Integrating Rights and Development. In Alston and Robinson, eds., *Human Rights and Development,* 297–326.

Gordenker, Leon, and Thomas G. Weiss, eds. 1996. *NGOs, the UN, and Global Governance.* Boulder, Colo: Lynne Rienner Publishers.

Goulden, Jay, and Sarah Glyde. 2004. *Development of a Rights Based Monitoring Tool for CARE Malawi.* London: CARE International UK. On file with author.

Goulet, Denis. 2002. A Christian NGO Faces Globalization. In *Local Ownership Global Change: Will Civil Society Save the World?* ed. Roland Hoksbergen and Lowell M. Ewert, 204–33. Monrovia, Calif.: World Vision International.

Gready, Paul, and Jonathan Ensor, eds. 2005. *Reinventing Development? Translating Rights-Based Approaches from Theory into Practice.* London: Zed Books.

Grusky, Sarah. 2001. This Is WATER We Are Talking About! GATS/Water: IMF Forces Water Privatization on Poor Countries. www.nadir.org/nadir/ initiativ/agp/free/imf/water.htm (accessed on May 11, 2004).

Guijt, I. 2004. *ALPS in Action: A Review of the Shift in ActionAid towards a New Accountability, Learning and Planning System.* ActionAid International.

Guilhot, Nicolas. 2005. *The Democracy Makers, Human Rights and the Politics of Global Order.* New York: Columbia University Press.

Hall, David, Kate Bayliss, and Emanuele Lobina. 2002. Water Privatisation in Africa. Presented at Municipal Services Project Conference, Witswatersrand University, Johannesburg, May 2002. www.psiru.org/reports/ 2002-06-W-Africa.doc (accessed on June 14, 2005).

Hannan, M. T., and J. Freeman. 1989. Organizations and Social Structure. In *Organizational Ecology.* Cambridge, Mass.: Harvard University Press.

Harris-Curtis, Emma, Oscar Marleyn, and Oliver Bakewell, 2005. The Implications for Northern NGOs of Adopting Rights-Based Approaches. Occasional Papers Series No. 41. Oxford: International NGO Training and Research Centre.

Health GAP. 2006. Global Access Project. www.healthgap.org/index.html (accessed on August 20, 2006).

Held, David. 2004. *Global Covenant.* London: Polity Press.

HERA. 1999. Confounding the Critics: Cairo Five Years On. www.iwhc.org/resources/confoundingcritics.cfm (accessed on August 1, 2006).

————. n.d. HERA: Health, Empowerment, Rights and Accountability. www.iwhc.org/global/un/unhistory/hera.cfm

Hertel, Shareen. 2006. Why Bother? Measuring Economic Rights: The Research Agenda. *International Studies Perspectives* 7: 215–30.

Hoering, Uwe, and Ann Kathrin Schneider. 2004. *King Customer? The World Bank's "New" Water and Its Implementation in India and Sri Lanka.* Stuttgart: Brot für die Welt and World Economy, Ecology and Development. www2.weed-online.org/uploads/KingCustomer_engl.fullversion (accessed on February 6, 2006).

Horta, Korinna. 1998. Letter to James Wolfensohn, President of the World Bank, September 1998. www.transcend.org/t_database/articles.php?ida =515 (accessed on September 22, 2006).

Hulme, David, and Michael Edwards, eds. 1997. *NGOs, States and Donors: Too Close for Comfort?* New York: St. Martin's in association with Save the Children.

Human Rights Council of Australia. 1998. *The Rights Way to Development: A Human Rights Approach to Development Assistance.* Sydney: Human Rights Council of Australia.

————. 2000. *Working Together. The Human Rights Based Approach to Development Cooperation,* Stockholm Workshop. October 16–19, 2000: 36–38.

Human Rights Watch, 1990. Ghana: Official Attacks on Religious Freedom. Human Rights Watch. Index: 0-929692-75-8 HRW, November 1, 1990. www.hrw.org/reports/pdfs/g/ghana/ghana905.pdf

————. 1995. Neither Jobs nor Justice: State Discrimination against Women in Russia. March 1995. www.hrw.org/reports/1995/Russia2a.htm

————. 1999. The Price of Oil. Corporate Responsibility and Human Rights Violations in Nigeria's Oil Producing Communities. www.hrw.org/reports/1999/nigeria/ (accessed on August 19, 2006).

————. 2001. *In the Shadow of Death: HIV/AIDS and Children's Rights in Kenya.* New York: Human Rights Watch.

————. 2002. HIV/AIDS and Human Rights. www.hrw.org/wr2k2/hivaids .html (accessed on May 10, 2004).

——. 2003. Women's Property Rights: Violations Doom Equality and Development. www.hrw.org/campaigns/women/property/ (accessed on May 10, 2004).

——. 2005. *Amicus Curiae* brief filed in DKT International v. USAID on November 15, 2005. http://hrw.org/pub/amicusbriefs/dkt_osi_110905.pdf (accessed on September 19, 2006).

——. n.d. Business and Human Rights, Documents. http://hrw.org/doc/?t=corporations&document_limit=0,20 (accessed on August 1, 2006).

Imhof, Aviva. 1997. Letter to Mr. Mitsuo Sato, President of ADB, from the International Rivers Network. October 29.

InterAction. 2003. Discussion on the Rights-based Approach to Development. December 17, 2003. In the offices of InterAction. At www.Interaction.org.

International Covenant on Economic, Social and Cultural Rights. n.d. Adopted and Opened for signature, ratification and accession by General Assembly Resolution 2200A (XXI) on 16 December 1966. www.unhchr.ch/html/menu3/b/a_cescr.htm (accessed on May 14, 2004).

International Finance Corporation. n.d. Fact Sheet on Chad-Cameroon Pipeline. www.ifc.org/ifcext/eir.nsf/AttachmentsByTitle/ChadCameroon Pipeline1/$FILE/CHAD+CAMEROON+PIPELINE+FACT+SHEET.pdf (accessed on September 19, 2006).

International Human Rights Internship Program and Asian Forum for Human Rights and Development. 2000. *Circle of Rights, Economic, Social and Cultural Rights Activism: A Training Resource.* Washington, D.C.: International Human Rights Training Program.

International Network for Economic, Social and Cultural Rights. 2002. About ESCR-Net. www.escr-net.org/EngGeneral/about_ESCR.asp (accessed on September 22, 2006).

International Right to Know Campaign. 2002. What Is IRTK? On file with authors.

——. 2003. *International Right to Know: Empowering Communities through Corporate Transparency.* Washington, D.C.: IRTK Campaign.

International Save the Children Alliance. 2001. *Annual Report 2001.* London: ISCA.

——. 2002. *Child Rights Programming: How to Apply Rights-Based Approaches to Programming.* London: ISCA.

International Water Working Group. 2002. Letter to World Bank President from the Ghana National Coalition against Privatisation of Water, February 19, 2002. http://www.citizen.org/cmep/Water/cmep_Water/articles.cfm?ID=7279 (accessed on May 14, 2004).

———. 2004. Water Is a Human Right, Say "No" to Prepaid Water Meters. www.citizen.org/cmep/Water/cmep_Water/ (accessed on June 16, 2005).

International Women's Health Coalition. 2002. Girls' Power Initiative. www.iwhc.org/index.cfm?fuseaction=page&pageID=325 (accessed on September 22, 2006).

———. 2004. Twenty Years, One Goal: IWHC's 20th Anniversary Report. www.iwhc.org/resources/20yearreport.cfm (accessed on August 3, 2005).

———. n.d.. The Human Rights of Children and Their Sexual and Reproductive Health. www.ippf.org/resource/meetings/unssc/pdf/factsheetseries/rightsofchildren.pdf (accessed on January 14, 2003).

Irvin, Andrea. 2000. *Taking Steps of Courage: Teaching Adolescents about Sexuality and Gender in Nigeria and Cameroun*. New York: International Women's Health Coalition. www.iwhc.org/uploads/ACF7DA.pdf

Isbister, John. 1998. *Promises Not Kept: The Betrayal of Social Change in the Third World*. 4th ed. West Hartford, Conn.: Kumarian Press.

Jochnick, Chris. 1999. Confronting the Impunity of Non-State Actors: New Fields for the Promotion of Human Rights. *Human Rights Quarterly* 2, no. 1: 56–79.

Johnston, Anton. 2000. Preparing the Swedish Country Strategy for Zimbabwe from a Democracy and Human Rights Perspective: Summary Report. In *Working Together: The Human Rights Approach to Development Cooperation Stockholm Workshop, Part 2*, ed. André Frankovits and Patrick Earle. Stockholm: Sida.

Joint Statement by NGOs on TRIPs and Public Health, 3 December 2005. www.cptech.org/ip/wto/p6/ngos12032005.html (accessed on February 6, 2006).

Jolly, Richard. 2004. Global Development Goals: UN Experience. *Journal of Human Development* 5, no. 1: 69–95.

Jones, Andrew. 2000. Rights-Based Relief and Development Assistance: An Essay on What It Means for CARE. In *Working Together: The Human Rights Approach to Development Cooperation Stockholm Workshop, Part 2*, ed. André Frankovits and Patrick Earle. Stockholm: Sida.

Jordan, Lisa. 2005. Mechanisms for NGO Accountability. Global Public Policy Institute Research Paper Series No. 3: Berlin. www.globalpublicpolicy.net/fileadmin/gppi/Jordan_Lisa_05022005.pdf (accessed November 21, 2007).

Jordan, Lisa, and Peter van Tuijl. 2000. Political Responsibility in Transnational NGO Advocacy. *World Development* 28, no. 12: 2051–65.

———. 2006. *NGO Accountability: Politics, Principles and Innovations.* London: Earthscan.

Keck, Margaret, and Kathryn Sikkink. 1998. *Activists beyond Borders.* Ithaca, N.Y.: Cornell University Press.

Keet, Dot. 1999. The International Anti-debt Campaign. A Southern Activist View for Activists in the "North" . . . and "the South." *Development in Practice* 10, nos. 3 & 4.

Khagram, Sanjeev. 2004. *Dams and Development: Transnational Struggles for Water and Power.* Ithaca, N.Y.: Cornell University Press.

Korey, William.1998. *NGOs and the Universal Declaration of Human Rights: A Curious Grapevine.* New York: St. Martins Press.

Laifungbam, D. Roy. 2003. The Human Right to Water: Necessity for Action and Discourse. Jubilee South. www.jubileesouth.org/news/EpZyVVlyFyg MevRBey.shtml (accessed on June 22, 2005).

Lawyers Committee on Human Rights. 1993. *Unacceptable Means: India's Sardar Sarovar Project and Violations of Human Rights.* New York: Lawyers Committee.

Levin, Tobe. n.d. Internet-Based Sources on Female Genital Mutilation. www.library.wisc.edu/libraries/WomensStudies/fc/fcwebfgm.htm (accessed on September 9, 2005).

Lewis, David. 2001. *The Management of Non-Governmental Development Organizations: An Introduction.* New York: Routledge.

Lindenberg, Marc, and Coralie Bryant. 2001. *Going Global.* Bloomfield, Conn: Kumarian Press.

Lustig, Doreen, and Benedict Kingsbury. 2006. Displacement and Relocation from Protected Areas: International Law Perspectives on Rights, Risks and Resistance. *Conservation and Society* 4, no. 3: 404–18.

MacDonald, David A., and Greg Ruiters, eds. 2005. *The Age of Commodity: Water Privatization in Southern Africa.* London: Earthscan.

Maddox, Perry, and Hanne Muller. 2003. *Sida and the Rights-Based Approach.* December 11, 2003. Unpublished typescript on file with authors.

Mandel, Stephen. 2006. *Debt Relief As If People Mattered: A Rights-Based Approach to Debt Sustainability.* London: New Economics Foundation.

Mann, James. 1999. *About Face: A History of America's Curious Relationship with China, from Nixon to Clinton.* New York: Alfred A. Knopf.

Manji, F. ed. 1999. *Development and Rights.* Oxford: Development in Practice.

Manteris, William. 2003. Center for Economic and Social Rights. Briefing paper prepared for the annual general meetings of Amnesty International USA, March 2003. On file with the authors.

Marks, S. 1981. Emerging Human Rights: A New Generation for the 1980's? *Rutgers Law Review:* 435–51.

Marvin, Simon, Nina Laurie, and Mark Napier. 2001. Pre-Payment: Emerging Pathways to Water Services. www.aguabolivia.org/newcastle/documentos/Nina-Marvin-southAfrica.htm (accessed on June 22, 2005).

Matas, David. n.d. *The Amnesty Mandate History.* Unpublished typescript, copy on file with authors.

Matthews, Jessica. 1997. Power Shift. *Foreign Affairs* (January).

Maung, Zara. 2006. Africa's Conflict Diamonds: Fair Trade Stones on the Horizon? *Ethical Corporation.* www.minesandcommunities.org/Action/press1119.htm (accessed on September 22, 2006).

McCully, Patrick. 2001. *Silenced Rivers: The Ecology and Politics of Large Dams.* London: Zed.

Médecins Sans Frontières. 2001. *Pills and Pocketbooks: Equity Pricing of Essential Medicines in Developing Countries.* Geneva: Médecins Sans Frontières.

———. 2002a. What Is the Campaign? The Basic Pillars. www.accessmed-msf.org/campaign/pillars.shtm (accessed on September 22, 2006).

———. 2002b. Brazilian Generic Drugs in South Africa—The Background. 29 January 2002. www.accessmed-msf.org/prod/publications.asp?scntid=2912002103754&contenttype=PARA&

———. 2002c. April 19th 2002 Is a Bittersweet Celebration: AIDS Treatment Still Reaching But a Fraction of All Those in Need. Statement on 19 April 2002. www.msf.org/countries/page.cfm?articleid=F364B35A-3864-492F-876F3D1B150A9261 (accessed on May 14, 2004).

———. 2004. Millions Have a Drug Problem. They Can't Get Any. www.accessmed-msf.org/documents/campaignbrochure2004.pdf (accessed November 26, 2007).

———. n.d. The Campaign. www.accessmed-msf.org/campaign/about.shtm (accessed on August 9, 2006).

Mekata, Motoko. 2000. Building Partnerships toward a Common Goal: Experiences of the International Campaign to Ban Landmines. In Florini, *The Third Force,* 143–76.

Middleton, Neil, and Phil O'Keefe. 1998. *Disaster and Development: The Politics of Humanitarian Aid.* London: Pluto.

Milanovic, Branko. 2005. *Worlds Apart: Measuring International and Global Inequality.* Princeton, N.J.: Princeton University Press.

Mitlin, Diana, and Sheela Patel, 2005. Re-interpreting the Rights-Based Approach—A Grass-Roots Perspective on Rights and Development. www.sed.manchester.ac.uk/idpm/research/events/february2005/documents/Mitlin.doc (accessed on September 15, 2006).

Moghadam, Valentine. 2005. *Globalizing Women.* Baltimore: Johns Hopkins University Press.

Mosley, Paul. 1995. *Aid and Power.* London: Routledge.

Nadler, D., and M. L. Tushman. 1995. Types of Organizational Change: From Incremental Improvement to Discontinuous Transformation. In *Discontinuous Change: Leading Organization Transformation,* ed. D. A. Nadler, R. B. Shaw, and A. E. Walton, 15–34. San Francisco: Jossey-Bass.

Natsios, Andrew. 2003. Remarks by Andrew S. Natsios, Administrator, USAID, InterAction Forum, Closing Plenary Session, May 21, 2003. www.usaid.gov/press/speeches/2003/sp030521.html (accessed on April 3, 2006).

Nelson, Paul. 1995. *The World Bank and Non-Governmental Organizations: The Limits of Apolitical Development.* New York: Macmillan and St. Martin's.

———. 1996. Internationalizing Economic and Environmental Policy: Transnational NGO Networks and the World Bank's Expanding Influence. *Millennium: Journal of International Studies* 25, no. 3.

———. 1997. Conflict and Effectiveness: Who Speaks for Whom in Transnational NGO Networks Lobbying the World Bank? *Nonprofit and Voluntary Sector Quarterly* 26, no. 4: 421–41.

———. 2002. New Agendas and New Patterns of International NGO Political Action. *VOLUNTAS: International Journal of Voluntary and Nonprofit Organizations* 13, no. 4: 377–91.

———. 2003. Multilateral Development Banks, Transparency and Corporate Clients: "Public-Private Partnerships" and Public Access to Information. *Public Administration and Development,* 249–57.

———. 2007. Human Rights, the Millennium Development Goals, and the Future of Development Cooperation. *World Development* 35, no. 12: 2041–55.

Nelson, Paul, and Ellen Dorsey. 2003. At the Nexus of Human Rights and Development: New Methods and Strategies of Global NGOs. *World Development* 31, no. 12: 2013–26.

_____. 2007. New Rights Advocacy in the Global Public Domain. *European Journal of International Relations* 13, no. 2: 187–216.

Nelson, Paul, and Srirak Plipat. 2006. The Turn toward Human Rights: Development Organizations and Rights. Paper available from the authors.

Newell, Peter. 2000. *Climate for Change: Non State Actors and the Global Politics of the Greenhouse.* Cambridge: Cambridge University Press.

Nussbaum, Martha C. 2000. *Women and Human Development: The Capabilities Approach.* Cambridge: Cambridge University Press.

O'Neill, William G. 2003. An Introduction to the Concept of Rights-Based Approach to Development; A Paper for Interaction, December 2003. www.interaction.org (accessed on September 22, 2006).

Offenheiser, Raymond C., and Susan H. Holcombe. 2003. Challenges and Opportunities in Implementing a Rights-based Approach to Development: An Oxfam America Perspective. *Nonprofit and Voluntary Sector Quarterly* 32, no. 2 (June): 268–306.

Ostrom, Elinor. 1990. *Governing the Commons: The Evolution of Institutions for Collective Action.* New York: Cambridge University Press.

Oxfam America. 2002. *Annual Report 2002.* Boston: Oxfam America.

Oxfam America and CARE USA. 2007. *Rights-Based Approaches Learning Project.* Boston: Oxfam Publishing.

Oxfam International. 2001. Dare to Lead: Public Health and Company Wealth. Oxfam Briefing Paper on GlaxoSmithKline. www.oxfam.org.uk/what_we_do/issues/health/downloads/daretolead.pdf (accessed on June 6, 2007).

_____. 2002a. 5 Aims. www.oxfam.org/en/files/annual_report_2000.pdf (accessed on September 22, 2006).

_____. 2002b. *The Right to Medicines, or the Right to Profit from Medicines.* Press release, November 12, 2002, on file with the authors.

_____. 2002c. *Formula for Fairness: Patient Rights before Patent Rights.* Oxfam briefing paper on Pfizer. www.oxfamamerica.org/newsandpublications/publications/briefing_papers/art793.html

PANNA. 2005. World Bank Monitoring: Campaign Materials. www.panna.org/campaigns/worldBank.html (accessed on September 9, 2005).

Pant, Ruchi. 2003. *From Communities Hands to MNCs' BOOTs: A Case Study from India on Right to Water.* Right to Water Project of Rights and Humanity, UK. www.righttowater.org.uk/pdfs/india_cs.pdf

Pattnaik, Jagat Ballabh, and Deepali Sharma. 2006. *Rights First* (April) www.actionaidindia.org (accessed on July 20, 2006).

Pécoul, Bernard, P. Chirac, P. Trouiller, and J. Pinel. 1999. Access to Essential Drugs in Poor Countries: A Lost Battle? *Journal of the American Medical Association* 281, no. 4 (January 27): 361–67.

Pfeffer, Jeffrey, and Gerald R. Salancik. 1978. *The External Control of Organizations—A Resource Dependence Perspective.* New York: Harper and Row.

Phillips, Michael M. 2003. The World Bank Wonders about Utility Privatizations. *Wall Street Journal*, July 21, 2003.

Physicians for Human Rights. 2003. Health Action AIDS: The Call to Action. www.phrusa.org/campaigns/aids/call.php (accessed on September 22, 2006).

Picard, Mary. 2003. Measurement and Methodological Challenges to CARE International's Rights-Based Programming. www.enterprise-impact.org.uk/pdf/Picard.pdf (accessed on September 19, 2006).

Picolotti, Juan Miguel, 2003. *The Right to Water in Argentina.* Report prepared for Rights and Humanity, November 5, 2003. www.cedha.org.ar/docs/doc175-eng.doc (accessed on June 29, 2006).

Plipat, Srirak. 2005. Developmentizing Human Rights: How Development NGOs Interpret and Implement a Human Rights–Based Approach to Development Policy. Ph.D. dissertation. University of Pittsburgh.

Pratt, Brian. 2003. Rights or Values? *INTRAC Newsletter,* no. 23 (January): 1–2.

Price, Richard. 2003. Transnational Civil Society and Advocacy in World Politics. Review article. *World Politics* 55: 579–606.

Publish What You Pay. 2005. Coalition Members. Updated June 24, 2005. www.publishwhatyoupay.org/ (accessed on August 5, 2005).

———. n.d.. Welcome to the Publish What You Pay Website. www.publishwhatyoupay.org (accessed on August 5, 2005).

Rand, Jude. 2002. *CARE's Experience with Adoption of a Rights-Based Approach: Five Case Studies.* June 21, 2002. Paper submitted to the CARE-USA RBA Initiative.

Research and Markets. 2006. *Water Deregulation, Ed. 2.* Dublin: Research and Markets.

Rich, Bruce. 1994. *Mortgaging the Earth: The World Bank, Environmental Impoverishment, and the Crisis of Development.* Boston: Beacon.

Rieff, David. 1999. The False Dawn of Civil Society. *The Nation*, February.

Risse-Kappen. Thomas. 1995. *Bringing the Transnational Relations Back In: Non State Actors, Domestic Structures and International Relations.* Cambridge: Cambridge University Press.

Risse, Thomas, Stephen C. Ropp, and Kathryn Sikkink, eds. 1999. *The Power of Human Rights: International Norms and Domestic Change.* Cambridge: Cambridge University Press.

Robinson, Mary. 2004. Advancing Economic, Social, and Cultural Rights: The Way Forward. *Human Rights Quarterly* 26, no. 4.

Roe, Emery. 1995. Critical Theory, Sustainable Development and Populism. *Telos,* no. 103: 149–62.

Roque, Atila. 2003. The Copenhagen + 5 Process and the Social Watch Experience: Notes for a Debate. www.fimcivilsociety.org/english/4-Atila _Roque-EN.pdf (accessed on September 22, 2006).

Ross, M. L. 2001. Does Oil Hinder Democracy? *World Politics* 53: 325–61.

Rostow, Walter W. 1960. *The Stages of Economic Growth: A Non-Communist Manifesto.* Cambridge: Cambridge University Press.

Roth, Kenneth. 2000. Human Rights and the AIDS Crisis: The Debate over Resources. Address delivered on July 11, 2000, at the XIII International AIDS Conference, Durban, South Africa.

———. 2004. Defending Economic, Social and Cultural Rights: Practical Issues Faced by an International Human Rights Organization. *Human Rights Quarterly* 26: 63–73.

Rubenstein, Leonard S. 2004. How International Human Rights Organizations Can Advance Economic, Social and Cultural Rights: A Response to Kenneth Roth. *Human Rights Quarterly* 26, no. 4.

Sachs, Jeffrey D. 2005. *The End of Poverty.* New York: Penguin.

Salamon, Lester. 1994. The Rise of the Non Profit Sector: A Global Associational Revolution. *Foreign Affairs,* July 1994.

Salamon, Lester M., Wojciech Sokolowski, and Associates. 2004. *Global Civil Society,* vol. 2. Bloomfield, Conn.: Kumarian Press.

Sano, Hans-Otto. 2000. Development and Human Rights: The Necessary, but Partial Integration of Human Rights and Development. *Human Rights Quarterly* 2: 734–52.

Save the Children Sweden. 2001. *Compass: Framework and Direction for Save the Children Sweden.* Stockholm: Save the Children Sweden.

———. n.d. Program Areas and Strategies. Stockholm: Save the Children Sweden.

Scholte, Jan Aart. 2004. *Democratizing the Global Economy: The Role of Civil Society.* Coventry: Centre for the Study of Globalisation and Regionalisation.

Schwartzman, Stephan. 1986. *Bankrolling Disasters: International Development Banks and the Global Environment. A Citizen's Guide to the Multilateral Development Banks.* Washington: Sierra Club.

Scott, John. 2001. *Power.* New York: Polity.

Scott, Richard. 1985. *Organizations: Rational, Natural and Open Systems.* Englewood Cliffs, N.J.: Prentice Hall.

Scranton, John, Angela Caesar, and Noémi Nemes. 2004. Water as a Human Right? Environmental Policy and Law Paper No. 51. www.iucn.org/themes/law/pdfdocuments/EPLP51EN.pdf (accessed on September 22, 2006).

Sen, Amartya. 2000. *Development as Freedom.* Oxford: Oxford University Press.

Sen, Amartya, and Jean Drèze. 1989. *Hunger and Public Action.* Oxford: Clarendon Press.

Shaw, Martin. 1994. Civil Society and Global Politics: Beyond a Social Movement Approach. *Millennium: Journal of International Studies* (Winter).

Simmons, P. J. 1998. Learning to Live with NGOs. *Foreign Policy* (Fall).

Sida. 1996. *Protecting the Rights of the Poor, Our Common Responsibility.* Stockholm: Sida.

———. 1998a. *Landanalys Zambia.* Zambia: Sida.

———. 1998b. *Country Strategy for Development Cooperation: Zambia: January 1, 1999–December 31, 2001.* Stockholm: Sida.

———. 2001. *Country Strategy Development: Guide for Country Analysis from a Democratic Governance and Human Rights Perspective.* Stockholm: Sida.

———. 2003. *Country Strategy for Zambia: 2003–2007.* Stockholm: Sida.

Slim, Hugo. 1997. To the Rescue: Radicals or Poodles. *World Today* (August–September).

Smillie, I., and L. Gberie. 2001. Dirty Diamonds and Civil Society. Prepared for the 4th CIVICUS World Assembly, August 2001, Vancouver, B.C.

Sogge, David. 1996. *Compassion and Calculation: The Practice of Private Foreign Aid.* London: Pluto.

South African Municipal Workers Union (SAMWU) & Rural Development Services Network (RDSN). 2002. Joint SAMWU-RDSN World Water Day press statement. www.worldwaterday.org/wwday/events/view.php?id=86 (accessed November 25, 2007).

Squires, John, Malcolm Langford, and Bret Thiele, eds. 2005. *The Road to a Remedy: Current Issues in the Litigation of Economic, Social and Cultural Rights.* Sydney: Australian Human Rights Centre.

Stammers, Neil. 1999. The Social Construction of Human Rights. *Human Rights Quarterly* 21, no. 4: 980–1008.

Stern, Nicholas. 2002. *A Case for Aid: Building Consensus for Development Assistance.* Washington, D.C.: World Bank.

Stoddard, Abby. 2003. With Us or Against Us? NGO Neutrality on the Line. Global Policy Forum. www.globalpolicy.org/ngos/fund/2003/1200 against.htm (accessed on September 22, 2006).

Sustainability Review. 2006. Bechtel Drops $50 Million Claim to Settle Bolivian Water Dispute. Sustainability Review news release. www .sustainablereview.com/articles/article/2773752/41886.htm (accessed on January 31, 2006).

Tarrow, Sidney. 2005. *The New Transnational Activism.* Cambridge: Cambridge University Press.

Terry, Fiona. 2002. *Condemned to Repeat? The Paradox of Humanitarian Action.* Ithaca, N.Y.: Cornell University Press.

Theis, Joachim. 2003. *Brief Introduction to Rights-Based Programming.* Save the Children Sweden, August 2003. www.crin.org/docs/resources/ publications/hrbap/brief_intro_RBA.doc (accessed on September 22, 2006).

't Hoen, E. 2000. Globalisation and Equitable Access to Essential Drugs. www .twnside.org.sg/title/twr120c.htm (accessed on September 22, 2006).

Thompson, James D. 1967. *Organizations in Action.* New York: McGraw-Hill.

Treatment Action Campaign. 2005. Annual Financial Statements for the Year Ended 28 February 2005. www.tac.org.za/audit/audit6/auditYear EndingFeb2005.pdf (accessed on May 29, 2007).

Tvedt, Terje. 2002. Development NGOs: Actors in the Global Civil Society or in a New International Social System? *Voluntas* 13, no. 4: 363–75.

UNDP. 2000. *Human Development Report 2000.* New York: Oxford University Press.

———. 2005. *International Cooperation at a Crossroads: Aid, Trade and Security in an Unequal World. Human Development Report 2005.* New York: Oxford.

UNICEF 1998. *A Human Rights Approach to UNICEF Programming for Children and Women: What It Is, and Some Changes It Will Bring.* New York: UNICEF.

———. n.d.. Human Rights for Children and Women: How UNICEF Helps Make Them a Reality. www.unicef.org/pubsgen/humanrights-children/ humanrightseng.pdf (accessed on September 22, 2006).

United Nations Economic and Social Council. 2005. Review of the First United Nations Decade for the Eradication of Poverty (1997–2006), Commission for Social Development, 12 December 2005, E/CN.5/ 2006/3.

Uvin, P. 2002. On High Moral Ground: The Incorporation of Human Rights by the Development Enterprise. *Praxis* 17: 1–11. http://fletcher.tufts.edu/ praxis/archives/xvii.html (accessed on September 22, 2006).

———. 2004. *Human Rights and Development.* Bloomfield, Conn.: Kumarian Press.

Van Tuijl, Peter. 2000. Entering the Global Dealing-Room: Reflections on a Rights-Based Framework for NGOs in International Development. *Third World Quarterly* 21, no. 4: 617–26.

Vidal, John. 2003. Coke on Trial as Indian Villagers Accuse Plant of Sucking Them Dry. *The Guardian* (Wednesday, November 19).

Wade, Robert. 2003. What Strategies Are Viable for Developing Countries Today? The WTO and the Shrinking of Development Space. *Review of International Political Economy* 10, no. 4: 621–44.

———. 2004. Is Globalization Reducing Poverty and Inequality? *World Development* 32, no. 4: 567–89.

Wapner, Paul. 1996. *Environmental Activism and World Civic Politics.* Albany: State University of New York Press.

WARIPNET and Human Rights First. 2000. From Response to Solutions— Strengthening the Protection of Refugees through Economic, Social, and Cultural Rights. A Discussion Paper on the Economic, Social, and Cultural Rights of Refugees in West Africa, presented at the 51st meeting of the Executive Committee of the High Commissioner's Programme, Geneva, October 2000. http://209.212.64.43:777/archives/ arc_pubs/ResponseSolutions.htm (accessed on January 28, 2008).

Water Aid. 2003. New Roles, New Rules—Does Private Sector Participation Benefit the Poor? Briefing Paper, London, February 2003. www.wateraid.org.uk (accessed on September 22, 2006).

———. n.d. Human Rights Approach to Development. www.righttowater .org.uk/code/HR_approach.asp (accessed on May 14, 2004).

Water Observatory. n.d. Document archive. www.waterobservatory.org/ Library/listContent.cfm (accessed on May 14, 2004).

Weiss, Edith Brown, Laurence Boisson de Chazournes, and Nathalie Bernasconi-Osterwalder. 2005. *Fresh Water and International Economic Law,* Oxford: Oxford University Press.

Weiss, Thomas, and Leon Gordenker, eds. 1996. *NGOS, the UN, and Global Governance.* Boulder, Colo.: Lynne Rienner Publishers.

Welch, Claude E. 2001. *NGOs and Human Rights.* Philadelphia: University of Pennsylvania Press.

Willard, Tim. 2005. Guatemalan Government's Apology Leaves Unanswered Questions. July 25, 2005. http://upsidedownworld.org/main/content/view/63/33/ (accessed on August 1, 2006).

World Bank. 1994. *Governance and Development.* Washington, D.C.: World Bank.

———. 1999. World Bank Briefing Note on Social Funds, October 27, 1999.

———. 2005. *Global Development Finance, 2005,* Washington, D.C.: World Bank.

———. 2007. *Global Development Indicators 2007.* Washington, D.C.: World Bank.

World Conference on Human Rights. 1993. Vienna Declaration and Programme of Action. Part 1, para. 30, adopted by the World Conference on Human Rights, Vienna, 23 June 1993 [A/CONF.157/24 (Part 1), chap. III] www.unhchr.ch/html/menu6/2/fs25.htm (accessed on August 30, 2006).

World Health Organization. 2000. Right to Water. www.who.int/water_sanitation_health/rightowater/en/ (accessed on June 16, 2005).

———. 2003. The Right to Water. Geneva: WHO. www.who.int/water_sanitation_health/rtwrev.pdf (accessed on January 28, 2008).

World Health Organization, COHRE, and American Association for Advancement of Science. 2004. Manual on the Right to Water. www.foodandwaterwatch.org/water/manual.pdf (accessed on September 22, 2006).

World Vision International. 2002. *Protecting Children: A Biblical Perspective on Child Rights.* Monrovia, Calif.: World Vision International.

Yamin, Alicia Ely. 2005. The Future in the Mirror: Incorporating Strategies for the Defense and Promotion of Economic, Social and Cultural Rights into the Mainstream Human Rights Agenda. *Human Rights Quarterly* 27: 1200–1244.

INDEX

The letter *t* following a page number denotes a table. The letter *f* following a page number denotes a figure.

Lightning Source UK Ltd.
Milton Keynes UK
30 September 2010

160567UK00001B/99/P